pleasure gardens
garden pleasures

Germany's
most beautiful
historical gardens

pleasure gardens
garden pleasures

Germany's
most beautiful
historical gardens

Official joint guide of the heritage administrations

Baden-Württemberg
Bavaria
Berlin-Brandenburg
DessauWörlitz
Hesse
Rhineland-Palatinate
Saxony
Thuringia

SCHNELL + STEINER

With constributions by:

Baden-Württemberg: Anneliese Almasan, Hubert Wolfgang Wertz; Alfons Elfgang, Rosemarie Münzenmayer

Bavaria: Jost Albert, Kurt Grübl, Rainer Herzog, Stefan Rhotert, Manfred Stephan

Berlin-Brandenburg: Ragnhild Kober-Carrière, Michael Seiler, Gerd Schurig, Jörg Wacker

DessauWörlitz: Ludwig Trauzettel

Hesse: Mandy Baumgart, Gisela Claes, Kai R. Mathieu

Rhineland-Palatinate: Agnes Allroggen-Bedel, Jan Meißner

Saxony: Andrea Dietrich, Roland Puppe, Simone Ruby

Thuringia: Wolfram Hübner, Catrin Lorenz, Helmut-Eberhard Paulus

Translated by Dr. Yasmin Gründing (Univ. [ond.] through Wort Welt Translation Agency)

Bibliographical information of the "Deutschen Bibliothek" (German library)

This publication is registered by the German library in the German National Bibliography. Detailed bibliographical data are available in the internet at http://dnb.ddb.de.

1st Edition 2003
© 2003 by Verlag Schnell & Steiner GmbH,
Leibnizstraße 13, D-93055 Regensburg
and the respective heritage administrations

Planing, preparation and coordination:
Erdmute Alex (DessauWörlitz),
Barbara Spindler (Berlin-Brandenburg),
Thomas Wöhler, Kathrin Jung (Bavaria),
Public relations and communications team

Cover: Astrid Moosburger
Setting, lithography: Visuelle Medientechnik GmbH, Regensburg
ISBN 3-7954-1536-5
Printed by Aumüller Druck KG, Regensburg

Printed in Germany on 100 % chlorine- and acid-free, age-resistant paper

CONTENTS

Symbols

i Information

⊘ Opening hours

⊞ Museum shop

♿ Accessible to the physically handicapped

✕ Restaurants

DB Train connection

🅿 Parking facilities

🚌 Bus connection/tram

Editorial Note:

The opening hours stated are subject to alteration. Please contact the relevant telephone numbers or e-mail/Internet addresses for current information.
This also applies for publications and further literature recommended by the individual administrations.

WELCOME

Ten years after the foundation of the "Professional Association for Palaces, Castles and Gardens in Germany", the second edition of our first, successful, joint publication in four languages, *Time to Travel in Time to Germany's finest stately homes, gardens, castles, abbeys and Roman remains*, was issued in the year 2000. The success of this venture aimed at bringing federal cultural heritage closer to the public, encouraged us to publish a second guide of equivalent layout and quality, devoted specially to our "paradise on earth" – the gardens.

You may have heard of some of these significant German gardens, such as those in Dresden, Pillnitz, the garden ensemble of Dessau-Wörlitz, Sanssouci and Nymphenburg, from respective current reports by the media on political, sporting and recent tragic events like the German "flood of the century" of the Elbe and its tributaries.

But have you ever visited and experienced the uniqueness particular to each of these "glimpses of paradise on earth"? You would be amazed by the diversity of the artistic characters of the gardens, the abundance of flora and fauna, the role played by water as the "soul of the garden", and the wealth of culture and recreation on offer.

Stately homes and gardens representing works of art complete in themselves have been passed down to us from the royal dynasties. You may witness the artistic competition among the ruling houses for the most beautiful garden, the rarest plants, the most impressive waterworks and the most extensive programme in the course of your visits. You shall meet generations of master gardener families, trained in Italy, France, Holland and England, who in the service of both worldly and ecclesiastical princes, created and nurtured these visions of paradise on earth, implementing their knowledge and experience in various locations.

Let this guide inspire and seduce you to come and visit and you will be sure to benefit by the diverse experience. Please allow us, the Schlösserverwaltungen (Palace and Castle Administrations) of Germany, to offer you both our warm welcome and our assistance.

Staatliche Schlösser und Gärten Baden-Württemberg
Public Stately Homes and Gardens of Baden-Württemberg

Bayerische Verwaltung der staatlichen Schlösser, Gärten und Seen
Bavarian Administration of Public Stately Homes, Gardens and Lakes

Stiftung Preußische Schlösser und Gärten Berlin-Brandenburg
Berlin-Brandenburg Foundation of Prussian Stately Homes and Gardens

Kulturstiftung DessauWörlitz
DessauWörlitz Cultural Foundation

Verwaltung der Staatlichen Schlösser und Gärten Hessen
Administration of Public Stately Homes and Gardens in Hesse

Burgen, Schlösser, Altertümer Rheinland-Pfalz
Castles, Stately Homes and Ancient Sites of Rhineland-Palatinate

Staatliche Schlösser, Burgen und Gärten Sachsen
Public Stately Homes, Castles and Gardens of Saxony

Stiftung Thüringer Schlösser und Gärten
Thuringian Foundation of Stately Homes and Gardens

PROFESSIONAL ASSOCIATION FOR PALACES, CASTLES AND GARDENS IN GERMANY

Caring together for great gardening works of art in Germany

Objective of the Professional Association for Palaces, Castles and Gardens in Germany is the exchange of professional experience and development of publicly maintained joint projects of the Palace, Castle and Gardens Administrations. The "Schlösser und Gärten Verwaltungen" (Palace, Castle and Gardens Administrations) in Germany are institutions for the preservation, study, complementation and communication of a unique comprehensive, artistic and historical heritage. This heritage consists of buildings, museums, objects of art and entire artistic landscapes, particularly gardening works of art, to which this volume is dedicated.

Although often unrecognised, the gardens also represent complete works of art of special historical significance and high rank in the history of art, thus contributing to the characterisation of a country's cultural and artistic identity. The preservation of gardening works of art and parks is in the interest of the general public. Especially in these times of new ecological concepts where man is trying to develop a more up-to date and appropriate attitude to nature, gardens have gained special social significance.

Examination of the higher spatial relationships, topography and concurrent landscaping is indispensable for the comprehension of garden works of art as a whole. Essential for understanding, is dealing with the history evident in the garden, especially in terms of dynastic and territorial contexts.

It is therefore the task of the German Palace, Castle and Gardens Administrations to preserve, maintain and look after the entrusted public property buildings and associated gardens as a whole. This includes opening them up to scientific research, reconstructing and completing them, but also making them appropriately accessible to visitors, presenting and communicating them as general works of art of correspondingly high value.

The Palace, Castle and Gardens Administrations united in the Professional Association for Palaces, Castles and Gardens in Germany view themselves chiefly as public service institutions, with the additional objective of working economically. They operate under the presumption that cultural awareness and economic thought and action can be coordinated. Especially in times of growing tourism and steadily increasing requests for different utilisation with simultaneous cutbacks regarding financing and staff, it is imperative that professional prerequisites for the achievement of this task remain united in one single body. Depending on the structure of the general works of art to be managed, the Palace, Castle and Gardens Administrations work on the basis of their own scientific research regarding each particular monument to be preserved, with integration of relevant fields of activities and services, under one joint management. Overall responsibility includes taking charge of the following areas of activity:

– Constructional matters, which include architectural as well as associated fittings dictated by the history of the construction and preservation of historical monuments.
– Museum work, including research, making art historical and aesthetical records and complementation.
– Restoration work meaning conservation and restoration.
– Garden art as comprehensive garden and landscape conservation under the primacy of garden history and preservation of garden monuments.
– Public relations and communication, presenting publicity-related publications, conduction of guided tours, museum education, exhibitions, advertising and such like.
– Property management including preservation and growth of assets, adequate management and utilisation in accordance with preservation guidelines.
– In the course of their basic and further training work, the Palace, Castle and Gardens Administrations ensure the efficiency of their specific work procedures, as well as making a contribution to providing qualified skilled manpower for all fields of work.

Dr. Kai R. Mathieu,
Direktor der Verwaltung der Staatlichen Schlösser und Gärten Hessen

Chairman

Dr. Helmut-Eberhard Paulus,
Direktor der Stiftung Thüringer Schlösser und Gärten

Egfried Hanfstaengl
Präsident der Bayerischen Verwaltung der Staatlichen Schlösser, Gärten und Seen

Deputy Chairmen

Approach to historical gardens

A historical garden is created by means of a combination of architecture and plants, public interest existing therein for historical or artistic reasons. As such it ranks as a historical monument.

These are the words used in Article 1 of the Charter of Florence – the Charter of Historical Gardens of 15 December 1981 – to briefly define historical gardens and their significance to society. This constitutes an international guideline for dealing with these important cultural assets. These principles have been adapted for practical use by the Association for Historical Gardens in the book issued by the DGGL 'Historical Gardens in Germany – Caring for Parks in accordance with the Principles of Preservation'.

Historical gardens are always a dialogue with nature, while the treatment and conception of nature may vary greatly in character as expressed by Renaissance, Baroque and landscape gardens. In the context of natural and intellectual history, historical gardens are documents of their time and sometimes also of individual personalities, with a close interrelationship to the other arts, such as literature, painting, sculpture, architecture and philosophy. Being a spatial structure on the surface of the earth, they are accessible by movement, by walking around the gardens, and thereby also by a sequence of impressions gathered in a period of time. Working with the materials of nature, with growing plants, with earth and water, changing times of the day and seasons of the years, endows the garden artist and garden art with a complexity extending far beyond their own capacities. Inherent in this lies however at the same time, the potential for self-destruction, in the sense that nature constantly tries to destroy the well balanced interplay of spatial proportions, diversity and contrast, by growth and decomposition. A historical garden therefore requires the supervision and care of gardeners initiated into its character to ensure its continued existence.

A historical garden is a unique artistic and cultural human creation, permanently bound to one location and using predominantly living plants, i.e. the integration of nature in man's conception of art. This includes a deep understanding of their nature, development and progressive transformation. A great diversity of spiritual currents arising in the course of an epoch may be expressed in historical gardens. Each historical garden is unique in itself and irreproducible. Its special features and secrets are hidden in its substance, this being the primary basis of interpretation, with the aid of written and pictorial sources and archive material. In addition to the distinctive features of spatial arrangement, earth sculpturing and architectural features, the historical garden is characterised by a specific selection, combination and development of its plants. A historical garden is a self-contained complete work of art, although it consists of sections designed with differing intensity, which are meant to be experienced sequentially. There are no areas to be considered as unimportant, to be neglected or even separated. With their scenic production of nature and art, the initiators and creators of the gardens wanted to convey a message to the visitor. To this end, historical gardens speak with an insistent language of their own. However it is necessary to learn to appreciate them, and one may in the end derive more insight from this dialogue than the creators placed into the gardens to start with. The message of the garden needs to be conveyed to the actual or potential visitor of today. The willingness to preserve historical garden monuments must be promoted in each generation and society, based on the clear understanding of their significance and value.

This task is also formulated by the Charter (Article 25): *The interest in historical gardens must be aroused by all and any means suitable for asserting recognition of this heritage, making it more widely known and raising it in public esteem. Promoting scientific research, international exchange and distribution of information, scientific publications and popular presentations; encouraging regular opening hours of the gardens to the public, sensitisation to natural and cultural values with the aid of mass media.*

How should a historical garden be enjoyed and what may not be imposed on it?

The visitor shall use and enjoy the historical garden in accordance with its character and be perceptive to its inherent message! The best protection for a historical garden is provided by the users having a general understanding of its special features and being aware of the many ways of appreciating it in conformity with its character and message. Historical gardens are a unique enrichment of the quality of life, offering the opportunity to experience the artistic and intellectual wealth of epochs of the past, by empathy and varying degrees of understanding, in a refreshing and enjoyable manner. Perception arising from a completely different kind of lifestyle may also awaken awareness and be profoundly impressive; indeed, it may even be antagonistic. This applies for example to the perception of life and space of a modern person, who may derive an unconscious dialectic pleasure out of strolling around a Baroque parterre. Neglected care, misunderstanding or inability to recognise the nature of the historical garden may lead to wrongful consideration of the garden as just some green area, which may be used in a new, substance and image destroying manner, such as for barbeques, playing, cycling etc. It is often not actually misunderstanding but the great pressure of utilisation needs, which threatens the substance of historical gardens.

The demands of a growing population with increasingly demanding requirements to create new gardens with new functional purposes and new artistic expression are immanent for the preservation of historical gardens. Places with historically designated use, such as hedge theatres, salons and squares, may – as long as the commercial pressure of the masses does not exceed limitations – be desirable and appropriate locations for the arts such as theatre or music performances and literature recitals.

The substance of a historical garden must not be destroyed for the primary purpose of functional need under the pretext of its capacity for renovation. Even with extensive in-depth research efforts, a large part of inherent relevant information can only be passed on to the next generation unrecognised within its substance. Historical gardens, which have matured to be unique resources for mankind, may on no account be confused with leisure and adventure parks. The latter's marketing methods are quickly exhausted being constantly on the lookout for new thrills; and suchlike should find no place in historical gardens. An introduction of events alien and potentially destructive to the character of the respective historical garden cannot be permitted. A historical garden may never be misused as background for large events for which it was not created, such as festivals, mega events, riding tournaments, sport events, sales and marketing events – in short, the wrong events at the wrong location. It should be noted that in principle, a historical garden requires no event or animation foreign to its character.

The local residents of the areas around historical gardens, the owners as it were, should learn to become connoisseurs and enthusiasts who are able to visit the historical gardens on a regular basis at any time of day regardless of season, gaining individual experience of art, history and nature, time and space. Since historical gardens require lasting comprehension for their preservation, in contrast to quick and temporary economic success, endeavours targeting the generations to come are of utmost importance. This means conveying to teachers the unique chance of real life teaching by integrating historical gardens in the subjects of cultural history, history, natural history, plastic arts and literature. Publications such as this should make it possible to find, develop, support and increase the number of garden connoisseurs and enthusiasts. The museum shops of the palaces, castles and gardens could reciprocally offer a wide range of multi-language literature on garden art in Europe, thus promoting comparison, study and interest in garden-based travelling. A travelling garden enthusiast collects knowledge, insight and joy. Consumerism is replaced by reflection on life's deeper meaning and wise enjoyment.

The Palace, Castle and Gardens Administrations witness their historical gardens being threatened daily with destruction and disappearance by overuse, misuse and lacking resources for maintenance. This dire state resulted in the idea of developing a preventative book on the etiquette of dealing with historical gardens. The ingenious work 'The etiquette of human behaviour' by a baron known as Freiherr von Knigge published in 1788, has become the quintessence of human understanding and consideration in social intercourse, based on mutual benefit. These comments on the proper treatment of historical gardens are intended as brief basic principles of a similar nature, directed to those making use of the gardens, presuming them to be cultivated and aware human beings.

Michael Seiler

Baden-Württemberg

STAATLICHE
SCHLÖSSER
UND GÄRTEN

STAATLICHE SCHLÖSSER UND GÄRTEN
BADEN-WÜRTTEMBERG

PUBLIC STATELY HOMES AND GARDENS OF
BADEN-WÜRTTEMBERG

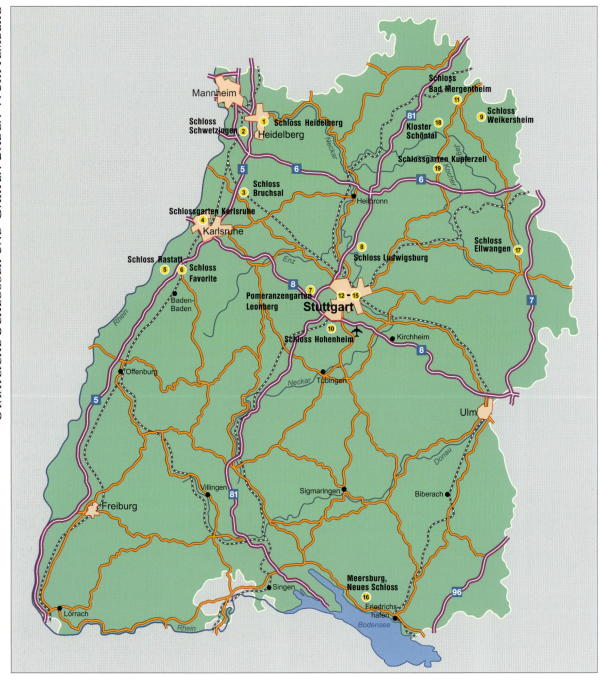

Heidelberg
  1 Hortus Palatinus (p. 16)

Schwetzingen
  2 Palace Gardens (p. 22)

Bruchsal
  3 Palace Gardens (p. 25)

Karlsruhe
  4 Palace Gardens (p. 27)

Rastatt
  5 Palace Gardens of the
    Baroque Residence (p. 29)
  6 Palace Park Favorite
    (p. 31)

Leonberg
  7 Seville Orange Gardens (p. 34)

Ludwigsburg
  8 Palace Gardens (p. 36)

Weikersheim
  9 Palace Gardens (p. 40)

Hohenheim
  10 Palace Gardens (p. 42)

Bad Mergentheim
  11 Castle Gardens (p. 44)

Stuttgart
  12 Wilhelma (p. 46)
  13 Rosensteinpark (p. 48)
  14 Palace Gardens (p. 49)
  15 Palace Square (p. 50)

Meersburg
  16 Palace Gardens (p. 51)

Ellwangen
  17 Gardens, Klausengarten
    und Wallgarten (p. 52)

Schöntal
  18 Monastery Gardens (p. 53)

Kupferzell
  19 Palace Gardens (p. 54)

◁ *Upper photograph:*
Palace Gardens Schwetzingen,
Natural theatre with Apollo temple

Lower photograph:
Stuttgart, Wilhelma

Old works of art as such are the property of educated humanity as a whole, their possession being associated with a duty to ensure their preservation.

Johann Wofgang von Goethe, 1799, quotation from the "Propyläen"

Hortus Palatinus, painting by Fouquière, around 1720/21

Whether on the upper Rhine or Neckar, on Lake Constance or in the Tauber valley, the Land of *Baden-Württemberg* enjoys an abundant range of garden works of art, usually incorporated in the ensemble palace, city and landscape of former secular and ecclesiastical residences. Initially planted by princes for themselves and the members of court society, they were opened up to the public early in their history, as is evident from the visitor regulations for the Palace Gardens of Schwetzingen from 1787: *His Electoral Excellency of Palatinate is not at all opposed to, but rather graciously disposed to kindly continue to permit free access to the large Stately Pleasure Ground of Schwezingen for every stranger or resident, no matter what rank.*

After centuries of being marked by the passage of time, the loss of original form. Sometimes redesigned beyond recognition, overgrown and exposed to destruction, threatened by disfiguring impacts imposed on their environment, these gardens have blossomed anew over the past decades. Reproduced with scientific accuracy, restored and partially reconstructed, and preserved in an exemplary fashion by the *Stately Homes and Gardens of Baden-Württemberg*, these sites of paradise created by man are once again available for the lover of art and the garden enthusiast in particular to submerge into a world of times long gone. What seems to be a Renaissance garden work of art placed immediately next to nature as divine creation, without any relation to natural landscape, seemingly complete in its own reality transcending nature, barely manifests itself in the Hortus Palatinus in Heidelberg, but may be appreciated in many ways in the Pomeranzengarten (Seville Orange Gar-

dens) of Leonberg. The 18th century creations of Baroque gardens in Weikersheim or Schwetzingen are products of exceptional garden art typical of the absolutist epoch. While the visitor passes through the grounds so thoroughly characterised by symmetry, past statues from the world of the gods of antiquity, the poetical idea of the return of the Golden Age is communicated by the gardens, enchanting with the abundance of Baroque decorative flowers and the scent of orangery plants, while simultaneously demonstrating the ruler's might and power over nature with the avenues and view axes to the landscape beyond.

Schwetzingen is also regarded as the nucleus of the English landscape gardens in southern Germany, with the extension of its grounds in the English landscape style in the second half of the 18th century. Gardens become paintings for walking in, with natural design of planting, paths and water features, romantic atmospheres created by means of grottos, artificial ruins or temples modelled on antiquity. The surrounding landscape completes and enriches the overall picture of grounds such as Bad Mergentheim or those of Favorite Rastatt.

Representing 19th century garden art, the Wilhelmina of Stuttgart with its exotic character, functions as a zoological-botanical garden today. The Botanical Gardens of Karlsruhe, with arboretum and extensive plant collections in greenhouses, also make garden dreams come true.

The gardens of Baden-Württemberg are well placed to convey to visitors a high level of enjoyable recreation and culture.

STAATLICHE SCHLÖSSER UND GÄRTEN BADEN-WÜRTTEMBERG

i Schlossverwaltung
Heidelberg
(Palace and Castle
Administration)
Schlosshof 1
69119 Heidelberg

🕐 Daily 8.00 am – 5.30 pm
Guided tour of the grounds
Daily on request in German
and English
Special guided tours on the
history of the palace and
gardens all year round and
on arragement by telephone
Service Centre
Tel. 0 62 21/53 84-31
info@service-center-schloss-
heidelberg.com
Schlosskasse
(Palace box office)
Tel. 0 62 21/53 84-21
www.schloesser-und-
gaerten.de

✕ Snackbar, Palace Restaurant

P Parking facilities

Hortus Palatinus – The unfinished eighth Wonder of the World in Heidelberg

*... and may the deed be proof of my humble,
sincerest and most passionate love.*
Extract of a letter dated 1 October 1612
written by Friedrich V to his bride Elisabeth Stuart

The Elisabethentor – a gate said to have been built over night - as a declaration of love by Friedrich V von der Pfalz (Friedrich V of the Palatinate) (1596–1632), hewn in stone for his beautiful wife on her 19th birthday, simultaneously marking the beginning of the Elector's biggest construction project: the creation of new palace gardens, the Hortus Palatinus – the Palatinate gardens. The splendour of the court and the elegance of the Heidelberg residence reached an unprecedented climax under the rule of Friedrich V, after the abundant jubilations on the occasion of the "dream wedding" celebrations marking his mar-

riage to the daughter of Jacob I, King of England. In order to provide accommodation befitting the rank of a King's daughter, but also out of the desire to be on a comparative level with the other European royal courts in terms of status and prestigious honour, the Elector had the entire palace grounds redesigned and enlarged.

The engineer, architect and scholar, Salomon de Caus brought along from England, started designing a new pleasure ground in 1614. De Caus, having been active at the English court and having travelled through Italy, proceeded to design a breathtaking conception of

Elisabethentor (Elisabeth Gate)

a Hortus Palatinus located on a steep mountain slope. It required extraordinary efforts by de Caus to build the grounds made up of two sections with five levels on four terraces divided into individual compartments, called parterres, on the sloping terrain. Elaborate and imaginative architectural creations were planned as garden decoration, such as a large grotto, a big tower-like belvedere, a double-sided hall with water pools for breeding fish, a large gallery with a small grotto, water basins and fountains with ingenious hydraulic systems, some of which were actually built. The portal of the Great Grotto, flanked by two obelisks, constituted the most striking feature of the entire grounds, and has been preserved until today. Thirteen animal figures – the lion as king of all animals and also as heraldic beast towering in the centre, as an allegory of the Elector of the Palatinate – decorated the arch.

Italian Renaissance gardens acted as model for this project in terms of ornamentation, and above all, with respect to the combination of nature, art and technology. The unfavourable topography demanded extraordinary powers of imagination of the garden architect in designing the compartments and grottos. The Hortus Palatinus may also be regarded as an example of a mannerist garden, in the sense that "a garden created by man comes immediately after nature itself, as a paradise on earth". On the threshold to the Baroque age, the Hortus Palatinus served as glorification of the ruling house, while simultaneously honouring the elements of nature. Friedrich had himself glorified as Apollo, god of muses, ruling over nature and the arts.

Election of Friedrich V to become King of Bohemia in 1619, also known as the "Winterkönig" (Winter King), and the relocation of his seat of government to Prague, resulted in the cessation of all work on the palace.

The portal leading to the Great Grotto, from an engraving by Salomon de Caus, 1620

Heidelberg Castle, aerial photograph

Although major parts of Salomon de Caus' ingenious conception were realised, the Hortus Palatinus famed as the "eighth wonder of the world" remained a mere fragment. Residual parts were converted into an English park in the 19th century – with an arboretum of magnificent individual trees, still preserved partially until today. The enormous efforts exerted by Salomon de Caus in terms of garden art, are not apparent at first glance, but become evident on closer inspection of the still existing terraces, ruins of stone buildings and reconstructions of several water basins and some sculptures, such as the one of the river god Rhein. His elaborate engraving from the year 1620 however manages to make this palace garden become alive again in everyone's imagination.

◁ *Statue of "Father Rhine"*

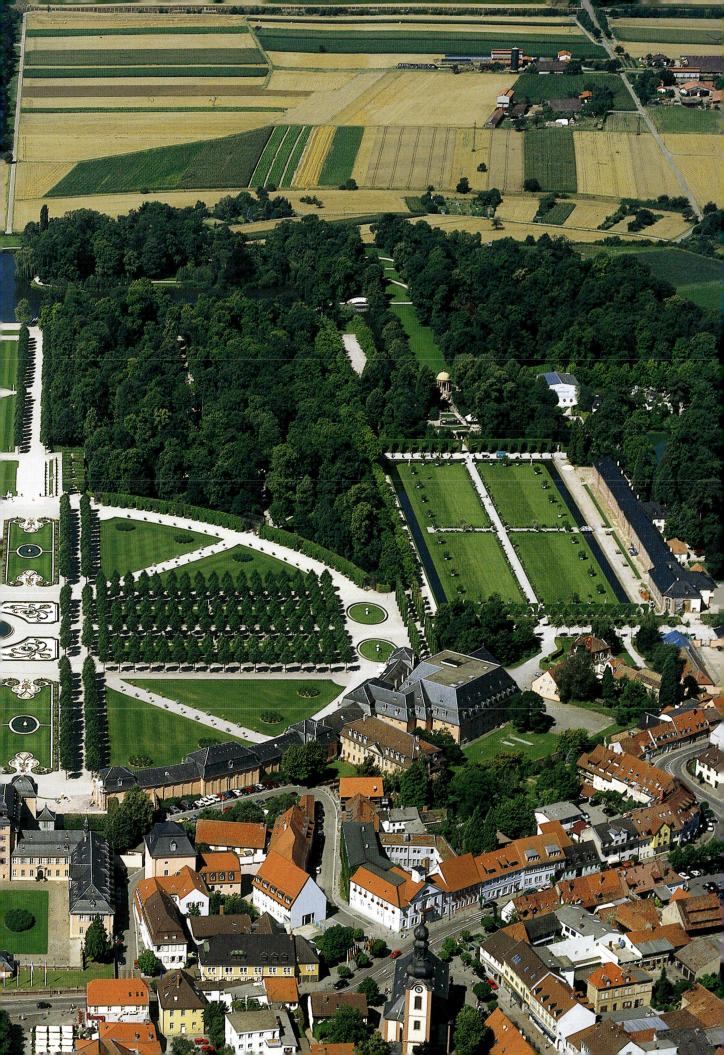

STAATLICHE SCHLÖSSER UND GÄRTEN BADEN-WÜRTTEMBERG

i Schlossverwaltung
Schwetzingen
(Palace and Castle
Administration)
Schloss Mittelbau
68723 Schwetzingen

🕐 Palace gardens all the year
round with admission
charge
Permanent exhibitions:
History of palace gardens in
the southern circle
History of the orangeries
and lapidarium (stone
museum) with original
sculptures in the orangery
"With spade, basket and
watering can ..." in the old
Baumagazin
(Building Store)
Special guided tours
on the history of the palace
and gardens all year round
and on arrangement by
telephone

Service Centre
Tel. 0 62 21/53 8431
info@service-center-schloss-
heidelberg.com
Schlosskasse Schwetzingen
(Palace box office)
Tel. 0 62 02/12 88 28
www.schloesser-und-
gaerten.de

✳ Palace café,
Palace Restaurant

P – **DB**

Palace Gardens Schwetzingen – Return of the Golden Age?

(...) dans le Temple d'Apollon il y viendra une Statue
en marbre representant Apollon debout tenant sa lyre de la main et
ayant à ses cotés des attributes de Poesie lyriques.
Nicolas de Pigage, 1765

Schwetzingen Palace Gardens, as an illusionary cosmos occupied by the Olympian gods, reflected the "Golden Age" in the 18th century: an age which had always represented the garden as a place of paradisiacal harmony protected by Apollo, god of the sun and Diana, goddess of hunting. Elector Carl Theodor regarded himself as the god Apollo, ruling over the muses and expressing his sense for the fine arts in Schwetzingen.

The history of the palace gardens of Schwetzingen however began much earlier. The Elector Carl Philipp of the Palatinate had a medieval Wasserburg (moated castle), which had been converted into a hunting and summer palace, enlarged, an orangery with central banqueting hall built, and a garden created with the help of the chief court gardener Johann Betting from Düsseldorf from 1722 onwards. A distinctive central axis in the shape of a

mulberry avenue connected Heidelberg with Schwetzingen, in accordance with the Baroque style of landscape design. In contrast, the garden enclosed from all sides, had the intimate image typical of the Italian Renaissance garden, the "giardino secreto".

Through the marriage with Elisabeth Augusta, the granddaughter of Carl Philipp, Carl Theodor took over goverment of the electoral Palatinate two decades later. As absolutist rulers with ambitions to power the passion of Elector and Electress was devoted to hunting and making merry at the summer residence in Schwetzingen.

Thus, Carl Theodor had Schwetzingen decorated with extensive gardens, circular houses with banqueting hall and theatre, instead of the old orangery, coupled by sumptuous embellishment with figures and waterworks. Notable architects

Previous double page:
Arial view of the entire grounds
of Schwetzingen Palace Gardens

Garden layout plan from 1806

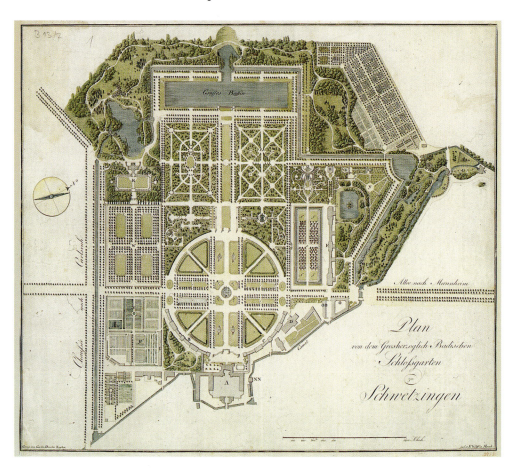

and masters of horticulture of the day, such as Alessandro Galli da Bibiena, Guillaume d'Hauberat, Johann Ludwig Petri and others, created a masterpiece of superlative Baroque garden art, based on Versailles as a model.

The most significant architect was probably Nicolas de Pigage, who entered into the Elector's service in 1749 as 'manager and artistic director of gardens and water displays'. In his function as director of gardens, he made significant contributions to the creative design of the Elector's representational gardens, which encompassed the entire area between the circular houses and the pergola walks, in the shape of a complete circular parterre. In accordance with the most up-to-date design methods based on Antoine Joseph Dezallier d'Argenville's French late Baroque garden theory, he established a stage for the social events of the court, amidst the near-natural surroundings created in the central garden parterre. A great diversity of ornamental flowers and broderies of perfectly geometrical topiary box trees, emphasised the severe axial division, with the Arion Fountain located at the point of intersection, endowing the gardens with an overall air of monumentality. Pigage built a new generously sized orangery for the ever-growing stock of orange trees.

Friedrich Ludwig von Sckell, who was won for the design of a new additional garden in 1777 under the chief supervision of Pigage, brought from England the

Garden parterre, water display

STAATLICHE SCHLÖSSER UND GÄRTEN BADEN-WÜRTTEMBERG

*Chinese bridge
with Mercury temple*

"natural" landscape style of garden for strolling in, which had already been known there since 1700. While the palace gardens including palace and city grounds represented an overall Baroque work of art, with their perfectly symmetrical and regular design based on clear mathematical patterns, the English landscape gardens represented a place for aesthetic and emotional experience, artistic and pastoral in expression. Moulded meadowland, quiet waters, apparently naturally grown clusters of trees, meandering paths with view axes and sparingly implemented architectural and artistic elements, created an independent, separate image of a world bathed in sentimental atmosphere.

The sequence of different epochs of style may be appreciated again today in the largely restored and reconstructed Palace Gardens of Schwetzingen. The natural theatre with Apollo temple, the mosque with praying aisles, the bathhouse with telescope, the Minerva temple, the Mercury temple or the "Temple of Forest Botany" and others, are all architectural staffages of exceptional beauty. Strolling through the parterres, the boskets, the "Angloises", the electoral private gardens, or the English gardens, one may discover sculptures in water basins, on planting beds or as eyecatchers at the end of avenues, heralding the poetic, imagined return of the "Golden Age" under the aegis of Apollo, while Pan the god of shepherds on a rock, symbolises the new feeling of natural freedom.

Palace Gardens Bruchsal – Home of sophisticated water displays

(...) is a pipe, which with your Excellency's most kind permission, with beautiful vexing water and a seat, on which should one sit shall be so wet himself until he shall stand up again.
From a letter by Balthasar Neumann to
Prince Bishop Damian Hugo of Schönborn

The questions with regard to closing the "hole in the middle", and "where the steps shall be placed", as posed by Prince Bishop Damian Hugo of Schönborn in a letter to Balthasar Neumann, were to be answered with the master builder's ingenious solution during his stay in Bruchsal in 1731. He personally made a model of the "main steps" of wood and gypsum and sketched designs for the vestibule, the grotto hall, the garden hall and the terraces on the court and garden side, as well as a clever "plan for a water pipe system" supplying water to the palace and gardens some years later. The palace gardens created in 1721, after establishment of the Prince Bishop's residence, orientated with strict geometry towards the long principal axis, were now finished with the heart piece designed by Balthasar Neumann. Neumann placed a grotto in the centre of the staircase, which is accessed via the vestibule – the intrada of the middle building, as a temple-like anteroom surrounded with pillars of Doric order.

A grotto was one of the features of a stately park in those days, being a room of mystery and representing the contrast between disorderly nature and nature fashioned by man, as expressed in the gardens. Adjoining this was the garden

i Schlossverwaltung Bruchsal (Palace and Castle Administration)
Schlossraum 4
76646 Bruchsal

⊙ Special guided tours on the history of the palace and gardens all year round and on arrangement by telephone

Service Centre
Tel. 0 72 22/93 41 70
Visitor centre /
Palace box office
Tel. 0 72 51/74 26 61
info@schloss-bruchsal.de
Palace gardens freely accessible
www.schloesser-und-gaerten.de

✕ Schlosscafé (Palace café)

P

DB S-Bahn (suburban railway)

Garden hall

hall – sala terrena – the vital link of every Baroque palace to terrace and gardens.

Placed on the axis of the side entrances, there were two circular basins fitted with fountains on the palace terrace leading into the gardens, the terrace being, just like the side terraces of the orangery building, an integral part of palace architecture. The large central basin with its enormous jet of water, lends formal splendour to the terrace. Stone figures of four halberds on the balustrade, fashioned by Joachim Günther around 1758, guard the grounds symbolically in their Spanish costumes. Access to the lower-lying gardens is surprisingly not by means of the broad steps typical of Baroque garden art, but via a little ramp leading onto the broad central axis. The gardens are enclosed by a dominating border of double chestnut avenues, opening up towards the palace in the shape of a "U". Lined up along the central axis today, are copies of group sculptures of the Four Seasons and the Four Elements representing the all-encompassing cosmos by their corresponding cyclic arrangement. Only remnants have remained of the Baroque garden design, with symmetrical planting beds, circular paths, avenues, sculptures, amusing water displays of fountains and water basins, which formed an artistic entity with the palace, and a stage for the glamorous festivities of the court in summer. The original garden sculptures of the Four Elements by Joachim Günther (1762) are housed in the garden hall today.

The palace gardens were restructured in the style of English landscape gardens in 1760, which has been preserved in the side parterres. A third phase of development gave rise to the romantic grottos near the Swan Pond of 1908, while a rose garden is situated to the north and a playground for small children is located to the south of the secluded large "Rondelle" at the lower end of the gardens.

Palace and gardens suffered severe damage during a bombing raid on 1 March 1945. The late Baroque residence was reconstructed and large parts of the central building were complemented in accordance with original plans, until 1975. Only the remaining upper section of the gardens was reworked thoroughly and planted with new avenues. The sophisticated water displays of the fountains, which have been put back into operation, have brought back an impression of former glory to the palace gardens.

Palace with Palace Gardens Bruchsal

Palace Gardens Karlsruhe – A green island in the fan-shaped city

BADEN-WÜRTTEMBERG

*Our only "plaisir" lies in the cultivation
of gardens and flowers.*
Margrave Carl Wilhelm
of Baden-Durlach

i 76133 Karlsruhe

⊘ Palace gardens, botanical
gardens freely accessible
Greenhouse with entrance
charge
Opening hours
April – September
Tues – Fri 9 am – 12 midday
and 1 pm – 4 pm
Sat, Sun and public
holidays 10 am – 12 midday
and 1 pm – 5 pm
October – March
Tues – Fri 9 am – 12 midday
and 1 pm – 4 pm
Sat, Sun and public
holidays 10 am – 12 midday
and 1 pm – 4 pm
Tours or special guided
tours only on arrangement
by telephone
Botanischer Garten
(Botanical Gardens)
Tel. 07 21/9 26 30 08
schlossgarten.ka@
tensionmail.de
www.schloesser-und-
gaerten.de

✕ Schlosscafe (Palace cafe),
Badische Weinstube
(Baden Wine Bar)

P

DB S-Bahn (suburban railway)

*Palace grounds and
Karlsruhe Palace*

When Margarve Carl Wilhelm of Baden-Durlach laid the foundation stone of his stately summer and hunting seat "Carols Ruh" in the Hardtwald, he felt a desire for rural seclusion and an opportunity to pursue his passion for gardening. The palace and extensive hunting grounds were declared as residence on 17 June 1715 and the foundation of the city was announced. A tower was erected at the centre of the perfectly formed circus, from which 32 avenues emanated radially. The palace was built within the nine "rays" directed towards the south, and in complete disregard of all Baroque rules of garden architecture, the pleasure ground was created in front of the palace rather than behind it. The central axis contained a magnificent principal and flower parterre, while four sunken gardens with flower and glass houses, aviaries and grottos lay adjacent to the sides. The Margrave entrusted the engineer and ensign of his guards Jakob Friedrich von Batzendorff, with the task of supervising the completion of the grounds. The gardens were neglected after Carl Wilhelm's death. Having been enlarged into a residence, the palace and gardens reached a new peak during the reign of his grandson Carl Friedrich and the artistically minded Caroline Luise.

The gardens were rearranged by skilled court gardeners and garden architects. This included their being reshaped into an English style park by Johann Michael Schweykert around 1800, with new botanical gardens, greenhouses and a court theatre designed by Friedrich Weinbrenner. The botanical gardens and all the greenhouses were modified again according to designs by Heinrich Hübsch during

STAATLICHE SCHLÖSSER UND GÄRTEN BADEN-WÜRTTEMBERG

Palace tower

the rule of Grand Duke Friedrich I (1852–1907).

The story of the palace and gardens came to a tragic end after removal of the palace nursery gardens in 1918, sealed finally by almost total destruction during the Second World War. The extent of this destruction can hardly be imagined thanks to reconstruction of the palace and gardens in the 50's and 60's of the 20th century.

The abundance of flowers and plants impress by their beauty, and the two round ponds in the middle of the gardens containing large carps and luxurious water lilies, are an attraction for even the youngest visitor. The exotic flair of the greenhouses rebuilt between 1952 and 1956, containing rare plants which, on account of their age, appearance or splendid colours, are a source of "plaisir" not only for the plant enthusiast.

Botanical gardens, greenhouse

Palace Gardens of the Baroque Residence Rastatt –
The Illusion of a Prince

Now Your Serene Highness ... upon my life ...
the whole world shall approve and say that this be one
of the most beautiful buildings not only in Germany, but also in Italy ...
Letter from the architect Domenico Egidio Rossi
to the Margrave dated 9 March, 1700

i Schloss Rastatt
Herrenstr. 18
76437 Rastatt

⊙ Gardens freely accessible
Hourly guided tours
of the grounds
Special guided tours
on the history of palace
and gardens all year round
and on arrangement
by telephone
Service Centre
Tel. 0 72 22/93 41 70

Visitor centre
Tel. 0 72 22/97 83 85
Fax 0 72 22/97 83 92
info@schloss-rastatt.de
www.schloesser-und-
gaerten.de

✕ Schlosscafe (Palace cafe)

P Bus parking area

DB S-Bahn (suburban railway)

Ludwig Wilhelm of Baden-Baden had planned a three-sectional complex as Jagdschloß (hunting castle) in the wide plains of the Rhine valley as early as 1697, with a small ornamental garden and a grand enclosure for animals to serve as convenient hunting grounds for the Margrave – "ad venationem commoditatem". Towards the end of 1699, the Margrave also known as Türkenlouis (Louis the Turk) on account of his victories in the battles against the Turks, abandoned the idea of Jagdschloss and decided to have an extensive residence with monumental palace built instead. His absolutist claim to power was to be expressed in the form of extensive gardens and a town consisting of model houses specified by plan and surrounded by fortification walls. The eager Italian immediately started with the realisation of the design, also creating sophisticated palace gardens appropriate for the dimensions of the palace building. Palace, park and town were positioned along a distinctive main axis connecting Ettlingen in the east with Fort Louis in the west.

The story of Louis the Turk who was celebrated in his lifetime and died shortly after completion of his residence, also applies to the palace gardens. The palace gardens, which were component of an overall work of art in a Baroque sense, were never finished. The efforts of his

Garden side, parterre

widow, Margravine Sibylla Augusta of Baden-Baden, were chiefly directed towards the creation of a new pleasure ground complete with summer and hunting palace near her residence – Favorite. The gardens changed hands several times in the course of the centuries. Their current design was created by the Swedish garden architect Gunnar Martinsson in the 80's of the 20th century. The new design realised by Max Laeuger around 1920, divided the gardens into three sections, incorporating the partially preserved conception of "modern age public gardens". The central axis was however not completed further. A green oasis in the middle of the Baroque town - the palace gardens today are a place for the recreation of all.

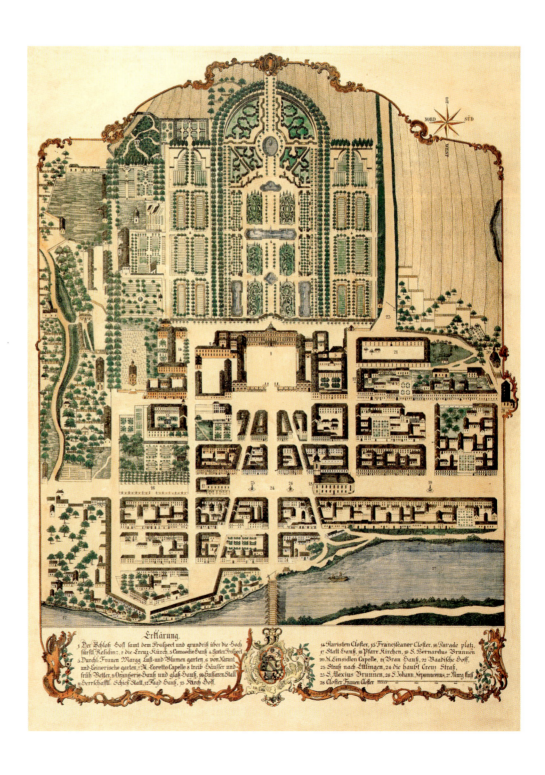

Ideal plan from 1798

Palace Park Favorite – The noble pleasures of hunting and festivity

A great attraction lies in the seclusion of palace and gardens.
They are set into the wide landscape like an island,
just like the island of Cythera, dream world of Baroque art and culture.
Rudolf Sillib

Margravine Sibylla Augusta of Baden-Baden could also not resist this charm. It was a combination of an increasing desire for idyllic seclusion in the countryside, the spirit of the times and her duty to represent, which caused the widow of Louis the Turk to commission the Bohemian master builder Michael Ludwig Rohrer with the construction of a hunting and summer palace near her residence in 1710. Building work on the palace had been completed by 1720, while work on the princely pleasure ground, the pheasantry gardens and the "garden house" was still in full progress. The basic layout of the "project" consisted of decorative and utility garden components typical of a Renaissance garden. The entire grounds however followed the formal French 18th century style of garden, as expressed by the strict symmetry of design, the placement of main and side avenues, and the emphasis of the central axis with pools and fountains.

The palace situated on a raised terrace, was located at the point of intersection of the main axis characterised by canal-like water basins, leading from the main façade of the palace into a "stately Favorite Avenue", and an avenue continuing into the pheasantry gardens through another parterre on the courtside. Dense pergola walks of elm trees "berceaux de verdure" provided shade "in the gardens flooded with light enhanced by mirror effects of the water surfaces". The numerous orange trees and other exotic plants were housed in orangeries, following the Rastatt residence procedure. The central Great Hall of the summer palace associated closely to the gardens by virtue of two gateways and geometrically designed parterres, provided a grandiose stage for the sumptuous enjoyment of court so-

i Schloss Favorite
Rastatt- Förch
76437 Rastatt

☉ Palace park freely accessible
Special guided tours on the history of the palace and gardens during the season and on arrangement by telephone
Service Centre
Tel. 0 72 22/93 41 70
Sightseeing:
Documentary account of the gardens in the terminal building of the orangery

Visitor centre
Tel. 0 72 22/4 12 07
Fax 0 72 22/40 89 57
info@schloss-rastatt.de
www.schloesser-und-gaerten.de

✕ Schlosscafé (Palace café)

P

Palace and Palace Park, aerial view

ciety, hunting balls, masquerades, joviality and amusement. The repentant widow had an Eremitage dedicated to St. Magdalene built in the middle of a dense spruce forest adjoining the gardens, for hours of religious solitude.

Schloss Favorite and its gardens became the much-loved summer residence of the lady ruler of Baden and her family. In 1771, the lack of male successors to the line of Baden-Baden, resulted in the margraviate territory being taken over by Margrave Carl Friedrich of Baden-Durlach who resided in Karlsruhe. Favorite Palace was demoted to the status of "stately country house" and the gardens were generally neglected. It took as long as 1788 until Carl Friedrich commissioned his court gardener from Pforzheim Johann Michael Schweykert with "the planting of a garden in the English style".

The strict geometrical architecture of the Baroque gardens was broken, and only the buildings, the octagonal fishpond, the gardens of the hermitage and the pheasantry forest were allowed to remain. An "undulating line of beauty" in accordance with the rules of design by Lancelot Capability Brown, may be observed on a picturesque long stretch of meadow with a naturally shaped pond and an island, which were created between the palace and the bridge to Kuppenheim. It was probably with an awareness of the design methods of the English garden theorist Humphrey Repton that Schweykert created an English park of exceptional beauty finished by 1805 and blending perfectly into the surrounding landscape.

The Baroque summer palace of Margravine Sibylla Augusta, which has survived in its original form, her quaint Eremitage, the orangeries, the cavalier houses and the extensive palace park in rural seclusion still possess an irresistible charm even today.

Palace Favorite, garden façade

Garden hall with a view to the court of honour

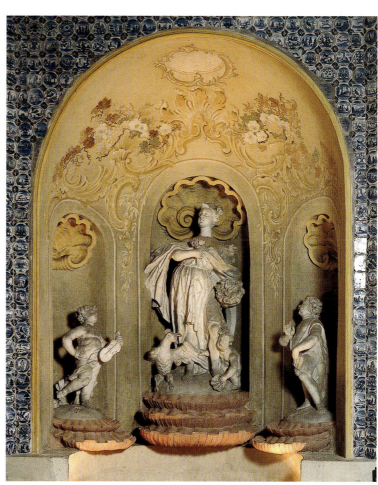

Garden hall, figure of Flora

Pomeranzengarten (Seville Orange Gardens) Leonberg

i Stadt Leonberg
Gartenamt
(Garden Authority)
Tel. 0 71 52/9 90 35 53
Fax 0 71 52/9 90 35 90

⊙ April – Sept.
8.00 am – 10.00 pm
Oct. – March
8.00 am – 6.00 pm

✕

P

DB

The terraces of the Pomeranzengarten jut out from a steep sloping edge below Leonberg Palace. Bordered with corner pavilions reminiscent of fortified towers, it still conveys the air of a Renaissance dream garden – a safe paradise distant from the real world.

It was created for Duchess Sybilla of Württemberg by Heinrich Schickhardt in 1609. The Land of Baden-Württemberg had it restored and reconstructed to its original form in 1980.

A colourful diversity of aromatic, seasoning and medicinal plants typical of that time, decorates the beds rhythmically organised as compartments and edged with railings. Solitary plants and fountains enhance this symmetry. The gentle patter of waterworks and the quiet scent of flowers and herbs transport the visitor back to times of royal garden pleasures long gone by.

The Seville orange, from which this garden derives its name, is a bitter orange. Recorded in Germany since the 16th century, in the Age of Antignity it was considered to be symbolic of the golden apples of the Hesperides, thereby suggesting the paradisiacal nature of the garden. This aspect is enhanced by the fountain motif – symbolising the fountain of Paradise, out of which flows eternal life.

As one of the few still preserved Renaissance gardens, it is a place of interest allowing the visitor to relive the elegance and beauty of garden art of times gone by.

*Aerial photograph
of the palace grounds*

Spring bloom

Corner pavilion and side fountain

Palace Gardens Ludwigsburg

STAATLICHE SCHLÖSSER UND GÄRTEN BADEN-WÜRTTEMBERG

ℹ Blühendes Barock GmbH
(Blossoming Baroque)
Mömpelgardstr. 28
71640 Ludwigsburg
Tel. 0 71 41/97 56 50
Fax 0 71 41/9 75 65 33

🕐 Mid-March – 31 Oct.
Daily 7.30 am – 8.30 pm
Märchengarten
(Fairy Tale Gardens):
Daily 9.00 am – 6.00 pm
Special guided tours
by prior arrangement
1 Nov. – mid-March
Daily 10.00 am – 4.00 pm,
only restricted accessibility

✕
🅿
DB

The palace of Ludwigsburg was built between 1704 and 1733, according to designs by the master builders Johann Friedrich Nette and Donato Giuseppe Frisoni. Its name originates from the founder, Duke Eberhard Ludwig of Württemberg, who moved his residence from Stuttgart to Ludwigsburg in 1718. The gardens established by him were reshaped and enlarged by his successors Carl Eugen and Friedrich. Today they are run by the company "Blühendes Barock (Blossoming Baroque) GmbH" as popular show gardens.

The **North Gardens**, under construction since 1708, originally determined the representational façade of the palace complex. It was intended to be a four-level terrace garden, but was never completely finished. Most of its significance was lost with the extension work yielding a four-wing complex from 1725 onwards.

The **South Gardens,** which are the largest, were terraced as early as 1708, being richly furnished with parterres and boskets. Design and size of the gardens was modified several times in subsequence of palace extension measures and changing representational requirements. The presentation today includes an extensive modern parterre divided by a cross-shaped arrangement of axes, the middle of which is occupied by a large oval late Baroque water basin.

The **East Gardens** are a very special treasure. In 1797, Duke Friedrich II had a landscape garden created on the grounds of an open quarry. The Upper East Gardens, representing the Age of Antiquity were counter faced with the Lower East Gardens, typifying the Dark Middle Ages. Modern Age was presented by the now remodelled Baroque gardens. The Upper East Gardens display a cheerful atmosphere as dictated by this iconography. Historical amusement facilities invite to stay a while: carousel, cabriolet and swing boats as well as a Russian wheel never fail to arouse the interest of children. A vineyard with a picturesque pavilion, a lake with shallops and parts of a ruin complement the scene. Once the playground was intended for adults once. The court bound by strict ceremonial was to be given opportunity for relaxation and unhindered social intercourse.

In 1990–92, the two **private gardens**, the Friedrichs- and the Mathildengarten, on both sides of the new Corps de Logis were restored according to the contemporary style of about 1800.

North Garden with the Old Corps de Logis

Lower orchard and Emichsburg

Friedrich's garden

STAATLICHE SCHLÖSSER UND GÄRTEN BADEN-WÜRTTEMBERG

Palace Gardens Weikersheim

i Schlossverwaltung
Weikersheim (Palace and
Castle Administration)
Schloss
97990 Weikersheim
Tel. 0 79 34/83 64
Fax 0 79 34/77 56

☉ 1 Apr. – 31 Oct.
Daily 9.00 am – 6.00 pm
1 Nov. – 31 March
Daily 10.00 am –
12.00 midday
1.30 pm – 4.30 pm
Special guided tours
by prior arrangement

*Previous double page:
Ludwigsburg, palace grounds,
with the south parterre and the
New Corps de Logis at the front*

Pleasure garden with orangery

The Palace Gardens Weikersheim represent a jewel of Baroque garden art in Hohenlohe, having largely retained their design until the present.

There is evidence of a count's pleasance and kitchen garden already existing in Weikersheim around 1600 to the south of the palace, including statues, exotic plants and a multi-level fountain arrangement.

Splitting up the inheritance in 1708 left Carl Ludwig of Hohenlohe with the ownership of Weikersheim. He enlarged the gardens significantly having them redesigned in accordance with the latest fashion. It is not recorded who designed the plans for execution, but it may be assumed that the master builder Johann Jakob Börel of Strasbourg was involved. The personal intentions of the Count inspired by his travelling impressions surely also found expression.

The Baroque idea is particularly evident in the symmetrical organisation, the festive parterre, the abundance of decorative figures, the great number of waterworks and a precious orangery, functioning both as winter quarters and festive hall.

The strong local character of the figures endows the work of art as a whole with an incomparable charm. Joie de vivre, imagination and humour are conveyed by this so very humanly fashioned gathering of gods, with whom the ruler associated himself allegorically. Courtiers and court servants – shrunk to the size of their significance – are getting together on the balustrade in an amiable affectedness.

View of the palace from the orangery basin

Orangery basin and orangery

Palace Gardens Hohenheim

i Hohenheim University
Tel. 07 11/4 59 20 01
Fax 07 11/4 59 32 89

☉ Open throughout the year

✕

P

DB

The palace grounds of Hohenheim are the largest of their kind to the east of the Rhine with a total length of 500 metres. Their history began with a medieval castle out of which developed a Meierhof (farm estate) and a Renaissance moated castle (residential castle surrounded by water) in the course of time. Duke Carl Eugen acquired the estate in 1768 and commenced with the initial construction of estate buildings in 1772. The architect was Reinhard Ferdinand Heinrich Fischer. Three representative palace wings concluded this building phase, which was initiated with the pulling down of the Wasserschloss in 1785. Interior work was not yet complete when Carl Eugen died in 1793.

Immediately facing the palace was a generous area, which also served as Cour d'honneur. The balcony of the entrance drive is located at the centre of the axes emerging radially from the palace. The adjacent representational gardens towards the south were designed as simple lawn parterre.

To the west of the palace, were the late Baroque grounds of the once famous "Dörfle" (village), which have become today's Exotic Gardens. Duke Carl Eugen and his wife Franziska created their own garden world here from 1772 to 1793 – a fantasy landscape filled with a picturesque abundance of antique, romantic and exotic park buildings and with a valuable collection of trees and shrubs from abroad. Most of the architectural features once created by the whim of the noble couple have disappeared, with the exception of a few remnants – the Playhouse, the so-called "City of Rome Inn" and the "Pillars of thundering Jupiter" – have disappeared. Remained has an extensive and spectacular park landscape with Botanical and Exotic Gardens.

An agricultural college moved into the palace in 1818, which developed into the University of Hohenheim in the course of time. The gardens were rearranged to suit teaching purposes. The systematic Botanical Garden were situated in the South Garden from 1829 until being relocated in 1974/76, and the "Dörfle" was turned into the Exotic Garden. The New Botanical Garden with the Monopteros were an addition to the southern area of the grounds in 1999.

Today, the entire grounds used by the University of Hohenheim are however also accessible to the interested public.

Pillars of Jupiter tonans,
gouache by Viktor Heideloff,
1800

View of the Exotic Garden from the herbaceous perennial garden in front of the Playhouse

Castle Gardens Bad Mergentheim

i Schlossverwaltung (Palace
and Castle Administration)
Bad Mergentheim
Tel. 0 79 31/5 22 12
Fax: 0 79 31/5 26 69

☉ Open throughout the year

✕

P

DB

The former, Deutschorden Hohenlohian (Teutonic order) Castle Bad Mergentheim originating from a moated castle, was elevated to residential level in 1527. The origins of its castle gardens go back as far as about 1600. The originally geometrically designed and frequently altered and enlarged grounds, were remodelled as landscape gardens from 1791 onwards by order of the Hoch- und Deutschmeister (High and Teutonic master) Maximilian Franz of Austria. Court gardener in charge was Franz Joseph Hüller. Work was carried out in three stages, paying tribute to agricultural (orchard meadowland), contemplative and representational requirements of the ruler. To the south of the central castle, yet within the castle moat, lay a spectacular garden hall (sala terrena) with an extensive orangery in a flower garden. The landscape gardens adjoined beyond the moat towards the west.

The Crown of Württemberg took over the property of the Teutonic order in 1809 as part of mediatisation measures. The extensive garden grounds were now opened to the public. Lacking or incorrect care lead to the dilapidation of the garden's contents in the course of time. The sala terrena and the flower garden disappeared completely. Restoration in stages of the 10 ha of palace gardens has been in progress since 1990.

As one of the most significant preserved landscape gardens of Baden-Württemberg, the gardens of Mergentheim display an enormous variety of creative design, as well as subtlety of design utilising light and space. Exotic motifs such as small houses known as the Schellenhäuschen at the edge of the arboretum and the Halbmondhäuschen in the middle of the orchard area alternate with generous landscape scenes. Mirror effects of the lake and memorial stones contribute to the rich atmospheric diversity featuring both cheerful and melancholic scenes.

"Schellenhäuschen" ▷

Poplar island

Wilhelma Stuttgart

i Wilhelma
Zoologisch-Botanischer
Garten (Zoological-
Botanical Gardens)
Neckartalstrasse
70376 Stuttgart
Tel. 07 11/5 40 20
Fax 07 11/5 40 22 22
www.wilhelma.de
info@wilhelma.de

⊙ May – Aug.
8.15 am – 6.00 pm
April – Sept.
8.15 am – 5.30 pm
March + Oct.
8.15 am – 5.00 pm
Nov. – Feb.
8.15 am – 4.00 pm

King Wilhelm I of Württemberg had already planned a bathhouse as retreat on the edge of the Rosensteinpark sloping towards the Neckar in the 30's of the 19th century, but was able to realise his dream only a decade later. In accordance with the fashion of the time, which associated exoticness with the idea of a bathhouse, the Moorish style was adhered to. He thus created an oriental fairy tale for himself and named it "Wilhelma". Officially opened in 1846, entrance was restricted to selected visitors on express permission by the King.

The grounds designed by the architect Karl Ludwig Zanth included a small residential tract of bicoloured sandstone, on either side of which greenhouses constructed of glass and iron were juxtaposed. The terraces bordering the flower gardens were surrounded by a colonnade and enclosed by a banqueting hall built in 1847–51 on the downside slope. A picture gallery and more glasshouses followed in 1853. A kitchen building and Damascene Hall complemented the grounds after Zanth's death.

The Wilhelma is characterised by a close association of private and representational rooms with greenhouses. Dual colour banded sandstone façades and modern constructions using the skeleton technique are combined in alternation with oriental decorative elements. The construction of rolled glass and richly ornamented industrial cast iron achieved a totally new kind of aesthetic approach. Light-flooded rooms with filigree outer casing are contrasted with colourful, sumptuously ornamented rooms with stone encasement.

The greenhouses were furnished with plants from the botanical gardens, including palms, azaleas, camellias, rhododendrons and orchids. They were primarily selected according to aesthetic criteria. 106 potted orange trees decorated the flower gardens in summer. A very special feature was the Victoria regia, the largest tropical water lily, generally unknown in Germany at that time.

After the Second World War, which brought the destruction of some of the buildings, exotic animals were housed in the gardens. Their enclosures and exhibitory houses – such as the bear enclosure, the predator's house, the hoofed animal grounds and the Amazonian house – were located around the historical centre. Today, the Wilhelma is a zoological-botanical garden of international repute.

Magnolia flowering ▷

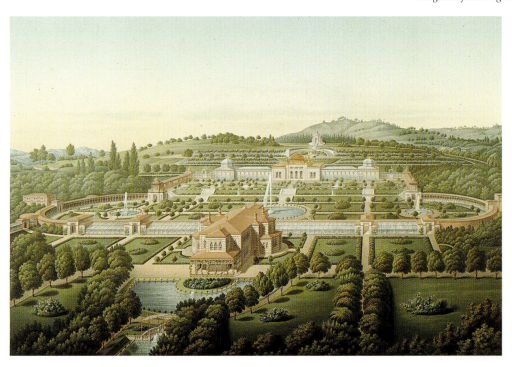

*Eastern view of the Wilhelma,
Ludwig von Zanth, 1855*

Rosensteinpark

i Tel. 07 11/5 40 21 23
  Fax 07 11/5 40 22 22

⊙ Open throughout the year

King Wilhelm I of Württemberg had a country castle built by Giovanni Salucci in 1823–32 on the hill jutting out above the Neckar, known as the Kahlenstein. The design and construction of the associated garden grounds in the English style was entrusted to the chief court gardener J. W. Bosch in 1823. Numerous designs by other notable architects had preceded this final choice. A generously sized classical landscape park was created. Accessibility was chiefly provided by a circular path, which passed densely planted borders, yet still allowed views of the surroundings beyond as well as of the inner park area divided by clumps of trees. Herbaceous perennials could be found mainly in the immediate vicinity of the palace and in the planted borders.

The Lion Gate with its two guardhouses was erected in 1834. The work on the park was finally completed around 1840. A pleasure ground, the Karlsgarten was added under King Karl in 1867 right next to the palace.

The park was however not merely intended for landscape beautification, but was also utilised agriculturally. The famous "Rosenstein cattle", a special breed of cow, was put out to pasture here. Grass from the neighbouring Wilhelma still serves as fodder for the animals today.

Despite the loss of large areas of land due to railway extensions, the railway post office, extension of the Wilhelma and so forth, the Rosensteinpark has managed to maintain its flair of generous expanse until today.

The classicistic palace Rosenstein in the landscape park

Palace Gardens Stuttgart

In 1806 King Friedrich, decided to beautify his royal capital by the creation of palace gardens. He commissioned his court master builder Nikolaus von Thouret with their design, sanctioning the plans with the remark: *so soll es seyn (it shall be thus)*. He handed over the gardens to his subjects in 1808 as a place for meeting and recreation. In this manner, the first public gardens of Württemberg came into existence in Stuttgart's meadow valley – a unique blend of traditional, geometrical and formal methods of design and the liberal element of the English style of landscaping. King Wilhelm I continued to extend the grounds all the way to the Neckar until 1816.

The palace gardens destroyed by war were rearranged for the occasion of the Regional Garden Show of 1961. The traditionally instituted procedure of the observer being presented with location, distance and idea prescribed by the ruling classes was not to be repeated here. On the contrary, open and festive areas for activities of a nature determined largely by the citizens themselves were to be created, interacting spatially with the surrounding architecture. This central theme, which also found expression in the utilisation of modern, industrially manufactured materials, refers to the basic attitude increasingly adopted in post-war Germany, namely to overcome the past in order to open the way for things new. A versatile garden of considerable artistic quality, open for public use by the citizens was created, whose design became a model to be followed by many German cities.

☉ Open throughout the year

⚔

🅿

DB

View from the Karlsgarten towards the Neckar meadows

Plane avenue with "Horse tamer" by Ludwig Hofer, Carrara marble 1848

Schlossplatz (Palace Square) Stuttgart

The genre of ornamental square or "Schmuckplatz" was developed in the 19th century from the idea of transferring garden functions to a square. It served for representation, cultural and ethical education of the population, improving the quality of urban life and expressing the divisions of society by means of differentiations in design. One of the earliest, most typical and beautiful of these squares was the Schlossplatz Stuttgart, which originated from a parade ground.

Its character was evident in the symmetry, the diagonally linked footpaths, the distinct spatial division, the carpets of beds as internal segmentation and the memorials and grandiose fountains.

The Schlossplatz continues to impress today by its expanse, spaciousness and characteristic features. It is a popular motif for photographs, the picturesque background for which is provided by the Baroque façade of the New Palace or the Königsbau (King's Building), erected in 1856.

Fountain "The Rivers of Württemberg" on the Schlossplatz

Palace Gardens Meersburg

A phantastic view of Lake Constance (Bodensee) and the Alps beyond the gardens offers itself from a terrace situated in front of the New Palace in Meersburg.

There is evidence of terrace gardens existing here as early as the 16th century. The gardens were designed in accordance with the latest fashion from 1712 onwards, after construction of the New Palace. Designs for palace and gardens were provided by the Benedictine priest Christoph Gessinger. A plan illustrating the situation existing in 1740 has been preserved, providing information on the lavish Baroque design. The gardens appear to float like a ship high above the lake by virtue of tall substructures. Placed in front of the main terrace, but notably lower, is another terrace on which an orangery used to be located. Although only parts of the exceedingly original and sophisticated garden features such as the ascending stairs and the tea pavilion on the lower terrace have been preserved, the gardens still impress with a breathtaking panorama even now.

i www.meersburg.de
info@meersburg.de
Tel. 01 80/5 63 37 72
oder 0 75 32/43 11-10
Fax 0 75 32/43 11-20

☉ 1 Apr.–31 Oct.
Daily 10.00 am – 1.00 pm
and 2.00 pm – 6.00 pm
Tour: as part of a guided
tour of the city or palace

✕ – P – DB

*View of the palace lakeside
façade and upper terrace*

The Gardens Klausengarten and Wallgarten Ellwangen

STAATLICHE SCHLÖSSER UND GÄRTEN BADEN-WÜRTTEMBERG

i Staatliches Vermögens-
und Hochbauamt
(State revenue and building
construction office)
Schwäbisch Gmünd
Tel. 0 71 71/60 24 72
Fax 0 71 71/60 24 59

Klausengarten:
Open all day

Wallgarten:
1 Apr. – 31 Oct.
Daily 8.00 am – 8.00 pm
Nov. – 31 March
Daily 8.30 am – 6.00 pm

The castle complex originating from the Benedictine monastery castle Ellwangen towers high above the city. The exposed location provides an impressive view of the hilly landscape of the Ostalb.

After abandonment of the old fortifications during the Baroque period, the Wallgarten and the Klausengarten were re-established. The Wallgarten is located to the south of the estate buildings; the Klausengarten is adjacent to the eastern buildings of the castle front annexe.

When Jérôme Bonaparte and his wife Katharina of Württemberg were given the castle as residence in 1815, the gardens were modernised. The Land Baden-Württemberg had the gardens restored in accordance with the old basic structural layout around 1990.

View of the pilgrimage church Schöneberg from the Klausengarten

Monastery Gardens Schöntal

The Cistercian monastery Schöntal founded in the 12th century was enlarged into a representative monastery complex under the abbot Knittel in the 18th century. The gardens, which have been preserved, are the Convent Garden, the Abbey Garden and a Parish Garden.

The Convent Garden was equipped with elaborate waterworks as early as the 16th century. Its central location directly behind church and monastery gave it significant representational importance. Baroque fountains, arrangements of steps and a linden tree pavilion bear witness to its great history until today.

The Abbey Garden, similar to the Convent Garden, combined practicality with beauty. Surrounded by a wall and arranged axially to the main entrance, it still displays orthogonal basic order, while the western orangery and the treillages dividing the garden into four compartments have not survived.

ℹ Bildungshaus
Kloster Schöntal
Tel. 0 79 43 / 89 43 11

⊘ Open throughout the year

✕

🅿

DB

BADEN-WÜRTTEMBERG

Convent Garden

Palace Gardens Kupferzell

i Staatliches Vermögens- und
Hochbauamt Heilbronn
(State revenue and building
construction office)
Tel. 0 71 31/64 36 33
Fax 0 71 31/64 33 63
Staatliche Akademie
für Landbau und
Hauswirtschaft Kupferzell
(State academy
for agriculture and
domestic science)
Tel. 0 79 44/29 01
Fax 0 79 44/29 32

In 1723 Count Philipp Ernst of Hohenlohe-Waldenburg-Schillingsfürst moved his residence to Kupferzell and had a palace built there. The Baroque palace gardens were significantly enlarged under Prince Friedrich Karl and transformed into a landscape park in 1840 except for a small parterre to the south of the palace front. Even today, the Feßbach brook and the large pond, the circle of oaks, the stag green, the peaceful Amalienruhe and the arboretum, bear witness to the beauty of this park embedded picturesquely in rural surroundings, while the luxurious orangery and the many vantage and shelter pavilions have not stood the test of time.

*"Amalienruhe" in the
Palace Gardens Kupferzell*

Source of illustrations:
Staatliche Schlösser und Gärten Baden-Württemberg
Kurpfälzisches Museum Heidelberg: p. 15
Landesmedienzentrum Baden-Württemberg: p. 16, 18, 23, 25, 26, 27, 32, 33
Stuttgarter Luftbild Elsässer GmbH: p. 19, 20/21, 31
Generallandesarchiv: p. 22
Stadtarchiv Rastatt: p. 30
Oberfinanzdirektion Stuttgart: p. 34
Birgit Maier, Calw: p. 35 oben
Alfons Elfgang, Weil der Stadt: p. 35 unten, 37, 53, 54
Landesbildstelle Baden/Steffen Hauswirth: p. 36, 40, 41 oben, 48, 49
Landesbildstelle Württemberg: p. 42, 46
Rosemarie Münzenmayer, Reichenbach: p. 43, 44, 52
Dieter Jauch, Stuttgart: p. 13 unten, 47

Bavaria

Bayerische Verwaltung der
staatlichen Schlösser, Gärten und Seen

Bavarian Administration of
Public Stately Homes, Gardens and Lakes

BAYERISCHE VERWALTUNG DER STAATLICHEN SCHLÖSSER, GÄRTEN UND SEEN

Ansbach
1 Palace Gardens (p. 58)

Aschaffenburg
2 Palace Gardens of Schloss Johannisburg (p. 61)
3 Park Schönbusch (p. 62)

Bamberg
4 Rose Gardens (p. 65)

Bamberg/Memmelsdorf
5 Palace Park Seehof (p. 66)

Bayreuth
6 Eremitage Palace Gardens (p. 67)
7 Bayreuth Palace Gardens (p. 70)

Bayreuth/Eckersdorf
8 Palace Gardens Fantaisie (p. 72)

Bayreuth/Wonsees
9 Rock Garden Sanspareil (p. 74)

Coburg/Rödental
10 Rosenau Park (p. 75)

Dachau
11 Palace Gardens (p. 77)

Eichstätt
12 Bastion Gardens Willibaldsburg (p. 78)

Feldafing
13 Feldafing Park (p. 79)
14 Rose Island (p. 80)

Herrenchiemsee
15 Palace Gardens (p. 81)

Holzhausen
16 Landscape garden of the artist's house of the Gasteiger (p. 84)

Ettal/Linderhof
17 Palace Gardens Linderhof (p. 85)

München
18 English Garden (p. 88)
19 Maximilian Park (p. 90)
20 Hofgarten (p. 91)
21 Palace Gardens Nymphenburg (p. 92)

Oberschleißheim
22 Schleißheim Palace Gardens (p. 95)

Veitshöchheim
23 Palace Gardens (p. 98)

Würzburg
24 Palace Gardens (p. 100)

◁ *Linderhof, view of the palace and terrace gardens*

Herrenchiemsee, southern marble fountain with lead-cast groups of hunting animals and marble sculptures of Amphitrite and Flora

THE GARDENS OF THE BAVARIAN PALACE AND CASTLE ADMINISTRATION

An extensive and diverse garden heritage has resulted from the long and chequered history of Bavaria. While gardens of Episcopal residences – Aschaffenburg, Bamberg, Würzburg and Veitshöchheim – and gardens of the regents of small principalities – Ansbach, Bayreuth, Coburg – are predominant in Franconia, the gardens of old Bavaria are chiefly those created by Electors and Kings of the House of Wittelsbach in Munich, Schleißheim, Dachau, Feldafing, Linderhof and Herrenchiemsee.

These reflect garden developments from Renaissance to Baroque and Rococo, all the way to landscape gardens of different character and historicising gardens.

Exceptional garden artists, architects and sculptors of the day were employed by Bavarian and Franconian initiators, such as Balthasar Neumann (1687–1753), Dominique Girard (–1738), Joseph Effner (1687–1745), Ferdinand Tietz (1708–1777), Friedrich Ludwig von Sckell (1750–1823), Joseph Peter Lenné (1789–1866), Carl von Effner (1831–1884). The activities of these artistic personalities have resulted in the creation of gardens, which represent milestones in the development of garden art. They are without exception, architectural monuments or components of monumental ensembles, according to the Law of Protection and Preservation of Monuments (preservation order) of the Free State of Bavaria.

Continued preservation and development of the gardens was placed in professional hands, as documented by the establishment of the Management and Artistic Direction of Court Gardens under the Ministry of Finance in 1804, making it possible to preserve many of the ancient garden works of art.

After the collapse of the monarchy, most of the stately homes, castles and gardens of the royal house, became property of the State of Bavaria, which initiated the "management of royal demesne" for looking after this cultural heritage. The "management of royal demesne" was renamed "Bavarian Administration of Public Stately Castles, Gardens and Lakes", which is in force until the present, being divided in four sections after the most recent reforms: central and landholding, museum, construction and gardens. The cooperation of all sections in one institution facilitates the preservation of the ensembles of monuments. Management of the gardens includes their preservation, their study and their complementation, as well as real-life conveyance of their historical significance. Under the Palace and Castle Administration in the whole of Bavaria are 17 Administration Subsections, responsible for organising the garden maintenance of 24 historical parks and 13 outdoor grounds associated with historical buildings as well as numerous lakeside areas, on site with the help of their own staff. The continuity achieved thereby, generally allows the fulfilment of the guidelines specified by the Bavarian Law for the Protection of Historic Monuments, "to maintain, to restore, to treat properly and protect from hazards".

Orangery with parterre

Ansbach Palace Gardens

i Schloss- und
   Gartenverwaltung Ansbach
   (Palace, Castle and
   Gardens Administration)
   Promenade 27
   91522 Ansbach
   Tel. 09 81 / 95 38 39-0
   Fax 09 81 / 95 38 39-40
   sgvansbach@bsv.bayern.de

   Size of the grounds: 18 ha

⊘ Park open throughout
   the year
   Guided tours of the park
   on request

♿ No restrictions

✕

DB

The Palace Gardens of Ansbach were first mentioned by Leonhart Fuchs, personal physician to the margrave from 1528 to 1535. In 1627, about one hundred years later, the court gardener at the time, first managed to get agaves to blossom north of the Alps. The palace gardens were enlarged into Baroque gardens during the period 1723 to 1750. Since the gardens did not directly border onto the Palace, an orangery designed by Karl Friedrich von Zocha in 1726–43 had to fulfil this function.

A decorative parterre flanked by two lime tree groves, was situated in front of the representational orangery. Major feature of the gardens was the 550 metre long avenue of four rows of trees, running parallel to the orangery. The gardens were severely damaged during the Second World War. The Bavarian Administration of Palaces and Castles has been engaged in efforts to restore lost elements and complete the range of historical plant stocks. The two lime tree groves to the side of the orangery parterre were replanted for instance. The framing borders are planted with a colourful multitude of spring and summer flowers each year, with inspiration from planting patterns of the 17th and 18th century. A remarkable stock of over 150 potted plants has been built up during the last decades, including lemon, Seville orange, olive, pistachio and strawberry trees. These decorate the area in front of the orangery during the summer months. Numerous monuments and commemorative plaques in the Hofgarten remind of famous personalities, including the botanist Leonhart Fuchs, the poet Johann Peter Uz and Kaspar Hauser, who met his death here under mysterious circumstances in December 1833.

Planting beds containing old seasoning and medicinal herbs as well as an assortment of rose bushes are on view in a separate area of the Palace Gardens. The modern Seville Orange House finished in 2002, has become a special decorative feature in this separate area of the gardens.

View into the great lime tree avenne

Rose gardens with new citrus house

Palace Gardens of Schloss Johannisburg

During the rule of the last Elector Friedrich Carl Joseph von Erthal (ruled 1774–1802) of Mainz, the four-winged Renaissance palace Johannisburg on the high bank of the Main represented an architectural highlight embedded in an extensive network of landscaped parks. The Elector started by having the landscape garden Schönbusch, followed by Schönthal in 1777 and the Zwinger (former moat), laid out as public gardens and promenades. The "breakfast pavilion" was erected in 1782, at the edge of the Zwinger and the palace gardens north of a Capuchin monastery. On a section of the old city wall, the "Capuchin path" leads from here to the oldest parts of the palace gardens of Schloss Johannisburg. The palace gardens were finally extended during the period 1843 to 1850, when King Ludwig I had the Pompejanum erected. The associated gardens (vineyard, peach trees, spruce forest etc.) were intended to present a Mediterranean landscape to match the building.

i Schloss- und Garten-
verwaltung Aschaffenburg
(Palace, Castle and
Gardens Administration)
Schlossplatz 4
63739 Aschaffenburg
Tel. 0 60 21 / 3 86 57-0
Fax 0 60 21 / 3 86 57-16
sgvaschaffenburg@
bsv.bayern.de

Size of the grounds: 6 ha

☉ 1. 4. – 31. 10.:
6.00 am to 9.00 pm
1. 11. – 31. 03.:
6.00 am to 7.00 pm

♿ Restricted due to steep
paths and steps at the
entrance of the palace

✕

P

DB

◁ *View of Palace Johannisburg from the Pompejanum*

Pompejanum and breakfast temple on the riverbank of the Main

*Carpet beds near
the kitchen building*

Electoral pavilion ▷

Kleine Schönbuschallee 1
63741 Aschaffenburg
Tel. 0 60 21/ 8 73 08

i Schloss- und Gartenverwal-
tung Aschaffenburg
(Palace, Castle and
Gardens Administration)
Schlossplatz 4
63739 Aschaffenburg
Tel. 0 60 21/ 3 86 57-0
Fax 0 60 21/ 3 86 57-16
sgvaschaffenburg@
bsv.bayern.de

Size of the grounds: 168 ha

⊘ Park open throughout
the year; Visitor centre
Schönbusch with exhibition
on the park:
April to September, on Sat,
Sun, public holidays
11.00 am to 6.00 pm
Guided tours of the park:
Information and booking
with the guide network
called "Führungsnetz
Aschaffenburg"
Tourist Information on
Tel. 0 60 21/39 58 00
Fax 0 60 21/39 58 02

⚿ No restrictions

✕ – **P** – **DB**

Park Schönbusch

The landscape park Schönbusch originates from a forest-like princely game
park, which the Prince Bishops of Mainz
had created about three kilometres to the
west of their secondary residence in
Aschaffenburg.
An enclosed terrain of about 81 ha, in
which mainly tame stags and pheasants
were kept, featured several straight aisles
and served as hunting grounds until
relandscaping was undertaken.
1775, one year after Friedrich Carl Joseph
von Erthal (1719–1802) was voted Elector, he commissioned his Minister of
State Friedrich Wilhelm von Sickingen
(1739–1818), with the restructuring of the
little forest, "Nilkheimer Wäldchen" into
a landscape garden, based on the English
model. In view of the ambitious enterprise, one no longer spoke of the Little
Forest of Nilkheim, but of the Beautiful
Bush or "Schönbusch". The buildings in
the new landscape garden were to be
designed and built by the Portuguese-

born architect Emanuel Joseph von
Herigoyen (1746–1817). Sickingen had
very concrete ideas as to how the old
game park was to be modified, and kept
starting arguments with the gardeners
working on site, or the architect Herigoyen and even the Elector himself, on
account of his contrary vision of how
things ought to be done. This may well
have played a role in the decision to
relieve Sickingen from his responsibility
for the artistic management of the restructuring around 1780 and transferring it
to the young garden artist Friedrich
Ludwig Sckell (1750–1823) of Schwetzingen. Sckell first developed a convincing
general concept for the rearrangement,
into which he wanted to integrate not
only the Schönbusch but the entire surrounding farmland. On the basis of this
plan the 1780's saw the creation of extensive park regions, large artificial water
areas, fine surface moulding and the
distinct meadow valley "Great Wiesen-

Red Bridge

tal" in the centre of the Schönbusch, traversing the park from north to south, until the present.

The Coalition Wars breaking out in 1792 after the French Revolution unfortunately prevented completion of the park. The capital Mainz and all of the Electoral State to the left of the Rhine fell to France. The end of the Electoral State Mainz was finally sealed with the general decision of the imperial deputation in 1803, just one year after the death of Erthal. The newly founded principality of Aschaffenburg was nevertheless ruled by Erthal's succes-

sors until 1814 in regional alliances of varying combination. After the fall of Napoleon, the region became part of the new Kingdom of Bavaria under Maximilian I Joseph. The Schönbusch came to be a royal Bavarian park and remained as such until 1918, becoming property of the Free State of Bavaria at the end of the monarchy. Since then, this remarkable early landscape park has been looked after by the Bavarian Administration of Public Stately Homes, Gardens and Lakes, being maintained with considerable financial expenditure year upon year.

Lower lake with "hills"
and observation tower

Rose Gardens Bamberg

The history of the rose gardens of Bamberg goes back as far as the last decades of the 16th century. A small Renaissance garden was situated at the site of today's rose garden then. Balthasar Neumann gave the gardens their symmetrical form in 1733, enlarging them to the area of the terrace still existing today. Hornbeams were planted alongside the balustrade on the city side. Visitors may enjoy a wonderful view of the city of Bamberg from here. Neumann made the remaining area of the garden accessible by means of an axial system of normal and circular paths – a basic structure, which has been maintained until the present. A circular fountain basin is located in the centre of the gardens and surrounded by trimmed lime trees. About 4500 roses grow in the box-bordered garden beds. Several figures also decorate the garden. Architectural focus of the approximately 4000 m² large gardens, is the dainty pavilion built in 1757, which houses a small café today.

ℹ Schloss- und Gartenverwaltung Bamberg (Palace, Castle and Gardens Administration) Domplatz 8 96049 Bamberg Tel. 09 51 / 5 19 39-0 und -114, Fax 09 51 / 5 19 39-129 sgvbamberg@bsv.bayern.de

Size of the grounds: 0.4 ha

⊘ April – Sept.: 9.00 am – 6.00 pm Oct. - March: 10.00 am – 4.00 pm, closed during winter if weather conditions are unsuitable

♿ No restrictions

✕

DB

Rose gardens

Palace Park Seehof

96117 Memmelsdorf

i Schloss- und Garten-
verwaltung Bamberg
(Palace, Castle and
Gardens Administration)
Domplatz 8
96049 Bamberg
Tel. 09 51/5 19 39-0
and -114
Fax 09 51/5 19 39-129
sgvbamberg@bsv.bayern.de

Size of the grounds: 21 ha

⊙ Park grounds open
throughout the year
Guided tours of the park
on request

& No restrictions

✕ – ℗ – ⅅⅅ

Lothar Franz von Schönborn, elected Prince Bishop of Bamberg in 1693, designated an area of 21 ha of land with adjacent lakes and forests to be made into gardens, axial to the yet unfinished summer palace. The Prince Bishop had the palace hill reshaped into precise terraces and the gardens divided into six large sections. He thereby created the garden structure that has remained until the present, which is exceptional in style on account of it being more reminiscent of Italian or Dutch parks, rather than the more customary French ideals. Prince Bishop Adam Friedrich von Seinsheim (1757–79) moved the cascade to the south and created a labyrinth. This was completed by the garden's decorative embellishment with 400 sculptures by Ferdinand Tietz, hardly any of which have survived until the present.

A chestnut avenue from 1797, used to lead beyond the enclosing walls to the Schweizerei (dairy) in the east and the pheasantry in the west.

The chestnut avenue and linden tree avenues framing the gardens and the "tapis verts", have been replanted during the last few years. Particularly impressive are the old hornbeam hedges along the main entrance driveway, the equally old pergola walk, and the lime tree groves.

Central to the garden is the cascade created in 1772, which dilapidated increasingly after secularisation and was put back into operation in 1995. Its programme heralds the glory of Hercules, in allegory of the Prince Bishop's glory.

Aerial photograph from the north

New and old palace

Eremitage Palace Gardens

Conversion of the Tiergarten (zoological gardens) founded in 1664, to an Eremitage commenced in 1715 under Margrave Georg Wilhelm (ruled 1712–26) with the construction of a summer palace as focus. Clipped linden tree groves grew adjacent to three sides of the four-winged complex by Johann David Räntz. A parterre was located before the banqueting hall, a cascade continuing from there all the way down to the Red Main river. Paths emanating from the wooded northern slopes lead to scattered hermit cottages, in which the 'recluses' secluded themselves to attain inner harmony. The access avenue is directed towards an artificial hill, the Parnass. From there, a pergola walk at right angles leads towards the palace.

The Eremitage was designed by Margrave Georg Wilhelm as a place for the theatrical imitation of hermit life. The margrave's court enacted the 'simple life' of a reclusive order.

Decisive for the continued development of the hermitage was the life and influence of the Margravine Wilhelmine (1709–58), a sister of Friedrich the Great. She received the Eremitage as a present from her husband Margrave Friedrich in 1735. The old palace was enlarged and several sections of the gardens were established, being characterised by water and architecture, such as the Lower Grotto and the Orangery Building (today the New Palace) with the Upper Grotto. In extending the park, Wilhelmine made use of traditional garden elements such as

Eremitage,
area St. Johannis
95448 Bayreuth

i Schloss- und Gartenverwaltung Bayreuth-Eremitage (Palace, Castle and Gardens Administration)
Ludwigstraße 21
95444 Bayreuth
Tel. 09 21 / 7 59 69-37
Fax 09 21 / 7 59 69-41
sgvbayreuth@bsv.bayern.de

Size of the grounds: 48 ha

⊙ Park grounds open throughout the year; waterworks from May until 15 October daily from 10.00 am until 5.00 pm; guided tours of the park and special guided tours by arrangement

⚹ Restricted in some areas due to steep paths

⚔ – 🅿

DB In connection with city bus

Parterre preceding the old palace

*Water display near
the upper grotto*

boskets, pergola walks and waterworks. Distancing from traditional Baroque gardens becomes apparent in the liberal arrangement of individual garden segments, the lacking central axis and the independence of individual sections from each other. Artificial ruins, like the ruin theatre or the margrave's hermitage, also contribute to making the Eremitage unusual as compared to other 18th century gardens.

The work-of-art gardens fell into decline after the death of the Margravine in 1758 and even more so after dissolution of the margraviate status in 1791. Regular features, wrought-iron work, vases and other decorative items were removed. Partial areas were sold. In 1823–37, Duke Pius of Bavaria spent the summer months in the Eremitage resuscitating the idea of reclusion for a while, and having a hermitage chapel erected next to the ruin theatre. King Ludwig II resided in the Eremitage during his attendances of Wagner's "Ring"-perfomances. Extensive reconstruction work was carried out after the Second World War, during which the New Palace was also severely damaged. Most of the sold-off pieces of land could be bought back and lost sections of the park were reconstructed. This included rebuilding the canal gardens, digging out and restoring the cascade buried around 1800, or reconstructing the wrought-iron work of the Upper Grotto. The summer flower border combinations based on 18th century principles and the numerous potted plant arrangements in summer, allow visitors to experience the 49 ha gardens very much as they must have been in the past.

Cascade

BAYERISCHE VERWALTUNG DER STAATLICHEN SCHLÖSSER, GÄRTEN UND SEEN

Palace Gardens Bayreuth

Schloss- und
Gartenverwaltung
Bayreuth-Eremitage
(Palace, Castle and
Gardens Administration)
Ludwigstraße 21
95444 Bayreuth
Tel. 09 21 / 7 59 69-21
Fax 09 21 / 7 59 69-15
sgvbayreuth@bsv.bayern.de

Size of the grounds: 14 ha

☉ Park grounds open
throughout the year
Guided tours of the park
on request

♿ No restrictions

✄ – ℙ

🚉 In connection
with the city bus

The gardens, which had already been property of the margrave dating back to the end of the 16th century, were reshaped and extended as of 1753, after construction of the new palace. The original plans for the Hofgarten (Palace Gardens) Bayreuth, attributed to court building inspector Rudolf Heinrich Richter, may be seen in the Museum of Garden Art Fantaisie. The maille alley avenue planted in 1679 was integrated in the new gardens. The avenue was originally planted with lime trees, then willows and alders, poplars in 1793 and ash trees in 1844, and finally oaks since 1943.

Adjoining to the south, the margrave and his wife had avenues, hedged-in sections, pergola walks and parterres created. A canal with four islands made up the central axis of the garden. Surprisingly, this axis bears no relation to obvious constructional features of the palace. The canal takes a right-angular turn before the end of the Hofgarten. A large Neptune group created by the brothers Räntz in 1763, which was to be placed on one of the islands in the canal, was never completed. Parts of this were set up in Park Fantaisie. Statues found in the building yard in the year 1889, were placed at various sites around the Palace Gardens. The gardens were overhauled in a "style characteristic of Engelland" at the end of the 18th century. Since then, paths meander

Palace canal with island

through liberally planted sections of the park. The basic outlines of the geometrical gardens are however still recognisable to this day.

A canal with a large island, as well as three main avenues and several gigantic trees dating from the 19th century dominate the character of the Hofgarten.

Several years ago, the area to the front of the city side of the new palace, with its promenade beneath topiary trees and flower ornaments to the side of the central margrave fountain by Elias Räntz, has been restored to original condition according to plans from 1864 by Carl Effner.

Large island with bridge

Bamberger Str. 3
95488 Eckersdorf/Donndorf
Tel. 09 21/73 14 00-11

i Schloss- und Gartenverwal-
tung Bayreuth-Eremitage
(Palace, Castle and
Gardens Administration)
Ludwigstraße 21
95444 Bayreuth
Tel. 09 21/7 59 69-75
Fax 09 21/7 59 69-15
sgvbayreuth@bsv.bayern.de

Size of the grounds: 17 ha

⊘ Park grounds open
throughout the year
Guided tours of the park
on request

Garden Art Museum –
April until September
9.00 am until 6.00 pm,
closed Mondays
closed October until March,

♿ Very much restricted due
to steep paths

✕

P

DB

Palace Gardens Fantaisie

"Fantaisie" – this was the name given by Duchess Elisabeth Friederike Sophie of Württemberg, the only child of the Margrave Friedrich and the Margravine Wilhelmine of Bayreuth to her summer residence in Donndorf. Here Friedrich had begun in November 1761 – three years after the death of his artistically minded spouse – with the construction of a new palace, alas, without living to see its completion. After her failed marriage to Carl Eugen of Württemberg, his daughter came to own the property in 1763. She had the palace finished and late Baroque gardens created until 1780. One pavilion, the Neptune fountain, supporting walls, stair constructions, fragments of a cascade and two original sandstone benches have remained intact from those days until today. The lost 18th century hedged areas to the east of the palace have been reconstructed recently.

Duchess Friederike Dorothee Sophie of Württemberg acquired the palace in 1793. She had the gardens enlarged in the sentimental landscape style. An abundance of charming staffages was created on the neighbouring forest slopes, a catacomb, the pillar of concord and various resting points, by integrating sandstone rocks found on site. Dorothee Sophie moved to Stuttgart in 1795, which interrupted the completion of the gardens. Being an offi-

Pillar of concord

cer serving in the Russian Army, her son Alexander Friedrich was not in a position to look after his inheritance as he might have wished. It was Duke Alexander of Württemberg who brought Fantaisie to new heights. He used the palace as summer residence from 1839 to 1881 and had it converted to its presently existing form in 1850/1852. This involved redesigning all façades in the so-called Florentine style. Duke Alexander however left many sections of the gardens unchanged. He also supplemented them with numerous design elements of pluralistic style, such as garden sculptures, fountains, pavilions and terraces – mainly however with landscaped park areas with many trees and shrubs from abroad.

Today Schloss Fantaisie houses Germany's first Museum of Garden Art. The history of garden art from the 17th to the 19th century is illustrated in real life by means of a varied sequence of representative areas. Valuable exhibits, including garden sculptures, paintings and graphics, porcelain and faïences, garden designs and models, gardening instruction circulars, garden furniture and gardening tools, convey the development of garden art, specifically in Southern Germany, in a visual manner. The palace park, uniting a smooth transition of original design elements from its three essential stylistic phases (Rococo, sensibility, historicism), is part of the Museum of Garden Art Schloss Fantaisie.

Palace Fantaisie with carpet beds

Rock Garden Sanspereil

Sanspareil
Haus Nr. 29
96197 Wonsees
Tel. 0 92 74/ 3 30 and 12 21

i Schloss- und Gartenverwaltung Bayreuth-Eremitage (Palace, Castle and Gardens Administration)
Ludwigstraße 21
95444 Bayreuth
Tel. 09 21/7 59 69-0
Fax 09 21/7 59 69-15
sgvbayreuth@bsv.bayern.de

Size of the grounds: 13 ha

⊙ Park grounds open throughout the year
Guided tours of the park on request

♿ Restricted in some areas due to steep paths and steps

✂

🅿

The rock garden Sanspareil is situated next to the medieval Hohenzollern castle Zwernitz, which Margrave Friedrich of Brandenburg-Bayreuth had renovated from 1744 onwards, while at the same time establishing the gardens.

At the sight of the rock garden in 1746, a lady of the court is said to have exclaimed: *"Ah, c'est sans pareil!"* – "This is without comparison!" which inspired Margrave Friedrich to order the renaming of Zwernitz to Sanspareil.

And in fact this is a very fitting name for the rock garden. Individual geometrical garden areas were embedded in an almost entirely natural forest environment, which features bizarre rock formations. Exotic-looking little lodges and country cottages were set on some of the rocks, which served as retreats for the "Eremitage Sanspareil". Many of these constructions dilapidated in the course of time and were sold "at demolition value" in the 19th century.

Still standing today however, is the ruin theatre, a mixture of grotto and ruin. The spectator area is located beneath an enormous natural rock arch, the orchestra pit, background, scenery wings and backdrop having being built with undressed rough stone. The Oriental Building and the Kitchen Building accommodating a café today have both been maintained until the present.

Around 1748, the caves and rocks were interpreted by Margravine Wilhelmine as Telemachian places, in accordance with a French educational novel – stations in the life of Telemachus, son of Odysseus, who, after a series of trials and adventures finally achieves "purification". The names of some rock areas, such as Calypso Grotto and Mentor Grotto remind of the literary programme of Sanspareil up to the present.

Castle Zwernitz and the rock gardens have been under the care of the Bavarian Administration of Palaces and Castles since 1942. The garden was restored in 1951 and the ground floor of the Oriental Building was reconstructed in 1987, according to a model engraving dating from the 18th century.

Parterre in front of the oriental building

Rosenau Park

Duke Ernst I of Sachsen-Coburg-Saalfeld had a 16th century castle converted in Neogothic style, and a landscape garden created in its surrounds from 1806. A leading role was played by the Duke's sister, Victoire von Leiningen, who was married by first marriage to the Prince of Leiningen, who had Amorbach Palace Gardens planned by Friedrich Ludwig Sckell, and by second marriage to the Duke of Kent. This explains why Rosenau displays both principles of design typical of Sckell, but also – particularly around the palace – romantic elements easily identifiable as English.

The sequence of different garden areas with varying views is supported by the natural terrain of the land, and it is not difficult to imagine how the 32 ha of core park preserved until today used to be an "ornamented farm" of 200 ha, incorporating the environment as part of the image of the park. The park presents varied scenes with its swan lake and paths lined with old trees running along the banks, a wide valley of meadows and steep slopes above the Itz with landscaped inclines.

Park architectural objects preserved until the present include the Neogothic farming house buildings, the classical teahouse and an orangery, today's Modern Glass Museum. Remaining decorative features of the park include the balustraded palace terrace, pavilion and fountain, grotto, tournament pillar, remnants of an artificial waterfall in the Itz and various stone benches, while the bathhouse and the fishing temple have disappeared.

Prince Albert, who married Queen Victoria of England in 1840, was born at Rosenau in 1819. The Queen visited Rosenau repeatedly, even after the death of the Prince Consort in 1861, holding it in high esteem: "... were we not who we are, this would be our true home."

Coburg was annexed to Bavaria in 1920, and the Bavarian Palace and Castle Administration took over the severely neglected grounds in 1972.

i Schloss- und Garten-
verwaltung Coburg
(Palace, Castle and
Gardens Administration)
Schloss Rosenau
Rosenau 1
96472 Rödental
Tel. 0 95 63/30 84-10
Fax 0 95 63/30 84-29
rosenau@sgvcoburg.de
www.sgvcoburg.de

Size of the grounds: 32 ha

⊘ Park grounds open
throughout the year
Guided tours of the park
on request

& Restricted in some areas
due to steep paths and
steps

✕

P

DB

Palace terrace with shallow bowl multi-tier fountain

Dachau Palace Gardens

After the badly dilapidated Castle Dachau was converted to a summer palace by Duke Albrecht V in 1558, a Renaissance garden designed in geometrical order with walls and square flower and herb beds, was created from 1578, based on plans by the painter architect Friedrich Sustris. It was the Elector Max Emanuel who proceeded to give the Palace Gardens of Dachau a Baroque image in 1715. The Elector's architect and master builder, Joseph Effner, replaced the flower and herb beds with two large broderie beds decorated with topiary box trees and flower borders. At the same time, the Elector ordered the purchase of a small forest area to the west of the gardens, which he and his successors filled with all sorts of playing equipment, including a skittle alley, a swing, various wooden huts and more. The gardens were simplified at the start of the 19th century. The general manager and artistic director of court gardens, Friedrich Ludwig von Sckell had fruit trees planted within the garden walls from 1802. The playing garden in the copse gradually disappeared.

Schlossstraße 7
85221 Dachau
Tel. 0 81 31 / 8 79 23
Fax 0 81 31 / 7 85 73

i Schloss- und Garten-
verwaltung Schleißheim
(Palace, Castle and
Gardens Administration)
Max-Emanuel-Platz 1
85764 Oberschleißheim
Tel. 0 89 / 31 58 72-0
Fax 0 89 / 31 58 72-50
sgvschleissheim@
bsv.bayern.de

Size of the grounds: 9 ha

⊙ Daily from 8.00 am until
dusk, but no longer
than 8.00 pm
Guided tours of the park
on request

♿ No restrictions

✕ – 🅿 – DB

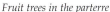
◁ *Pergola walk*

Fruit trees in the parterre

Eichstätt Bastion Gardens Willibaldsburg

BAYERISCHE VERWALTUNG DER STAATLICHEN SCHLÖSSER, GÄRTEN UND SEEN

Burgstraße 19
85072 Eichstätt
Tel. 0 84 21 / 47 30
Fax 0 84 21 / 81 94

i Schloss- und Garten-
verwaltung Ansbach
(Palace, Castle and
Gardens Administration)
Promenade 27
91522 Ansbach
Tel. 09 81 / 95 38 39-0
Fax 09 81 / 95 38 39-40
sgvansbach@bsv.bayern.de

Size of the grounds: 0.2 ha

⊙ Easter until mid-Oct.
9.00 am – 6.00 pm
Mondays closed
Guided tours of the park
on request

♿ Restricted accessibility;
there are no steps in the
gardens but very steep
inclines

✕

P

DB

Prince Bishop Johann Conrad von Gemmingen (ruled 1595–1612) instructed the architect and master builder Elias Holl (1573–1646) with the construction of the Willibaldsburg, seat of the Bishops of Eichstätt in around 1600. Today, this is considered to be one of the most spectacular testimonials of south German early Baroque. Gemmingen was however specially interested in his garden and its collection of plants. From 1592, the gardens were established in the immediacy of the castle by the physician and botanist Joachim Camerarius (1534–1598) from Nürnberg, and after his death, by the pharmacist and botanist Basilius Besler (1561–1629), who also lived in Nürnberg. Little is known of its exact location and design. Besler published the monumental copper plate engraving work "Hortus Eystettensis" in the year 1613, a florilegium, in which most of the plants growing in the Eichstätt gardens were represented diagrammatically on 367 copper plates and by 1084 individual illustrations. The florilegium is still impressive evidence of the scope of this early collection of plants even today. The Eichstätt Gardens were partially destroyed, but not completely ruined during the Thirty Year War. It was the cost-cutting measure of doing away with the last gardener position in the year 1795, which finally resulted in the demise of the once so famous botanical gardens.

Based on the precious copper plate engraving work, collection of the illustrated plants was commenced in the 1990's, with the aim of presenting them in the specially created "Bastion Gardens". This informative garden of about 2000 m² was opened in 1998. Planting of the individual beds is carried out analogous to the sequence in the horticultural book, according to the blossoming period of the plants. The first north-westerly bed features spring plants and the last south-easterly bed hosts the winter-blossoming plants illustrated by Besler. The plants on show in the Bastionsgarten originate from botanical gardens, plant cultivators and plant enthusiasts from both home and abroad.

*View of Eichstätt
from the Bastion Gardens*

Feldafing Park

King Maximilian II of Bavaria (1811–1864) chose the charming lakeside landscape near Feldafing on Lake Starnberg as location for his summer residence planned since 1840.

The royal Prussian court gardens director Peter Joseph Lenné was instructed to plan the park area in 1853. The King entrusted supervision of work to the young garden artist Carl von Effner.

Lenné's design of *"mixed" styles* intended terrace gardens descending immediately from the palace buildings down to the nearby lakeshore. Spun in a network of gently winding paths, this ensemble lay in a park landscape amid casually distributed groups of trees and shrubs. The well-designed interplay of winding paths, open meadows and planted areas, kept drawing one's view to the surface of the lake and the open landscape beyond. The untimely death of Maximilian II in March 1864 prevented the completion of palace and terracing. The park on the other hand was already finished by then.

Wittelsbacher Park 1
82340 Feldafing
Tel. 0 81 57/49 49
Fax 0 81 57/49 49

i Bayerische Schlösser-
verwaltung/Außenstelle
Starnberger See
(Bavarian Palace and
Castle Administration/
Lake Starnberg Branch)
Dampfschiffstraße 5
82319 Starnberg
Tel. 0 81 51/69 75
Fax 0 81 51/7 20 45
seeverwaltung.
starnbergersee@
bsv.bayern.de
Size of the grounds: 90 ha

☉ Park open throughout
the year; Guided tours of
the park on request

♿ No restrictions – 🅿 – DB

Glimpse of Lake Starnberg

Wittelsbacher Park 1
82340 Feldafing
Tel. 0 81 57 / 49 49
Fax 0 81 57 / 49 49

i Bayerische Schlösser-
verwaltung / Außenstelle
Starnberger See
(Bavarian Palace and
Castle Administration /
Lake Starnberg Branch)
Dampfschiffstraße 5
82319 Starnberg
Tel. 0 81 51 / 69 75
Fax 0 81 51 / 7 20 45
seeverwaltung.
starnbergersee@
bsv.bayern.de

Size of the grounds: 2 ha

⊘ Visiting the Roseninsel is
dependent on ferry service
Information on
Tel. 01 71 / 7 22 22 66
Guided tours of the park
on request

♿ No restrictions

P

DB

Rose Island

King Maximilian started his purchasing of land for the planned palace and park Feldafing with the acquisition of the fishing island Wörth in Lake Starnberg in the year 1850. It was to provide an opportunity for *"cheerfulness completely excluding all outside inquisitiveness,"* as an advisor to the King formulated its intended purpose. The Prussian court gardens director Peter Joseph Lenné planned the gardens around the small 'casino', which was built as summer residence on the small island between 1851 and 1853. Centrepiece of the gardens was a lilac-enclosed rosarium, where hundreds of tall-stemmed roses spread their delightful scent. Gently winding paths lead over the island through groups of trees and shrubs, often opening up to spectacular views of the Lake Starnberg. The romantic atmosphere and the seclusion of the island also won the favour of King Ludwig II, who enjoyed his sojourns on the Roseninsel (Rose Island), in the company of illustrious guests, including the Empress Elisabeth of Austria.

Rose island

Palace Gardens of Schloss Herrenchiemsee

Top priority was given to copying the palace and gardens of Versailles as an epitome of monarchic splendour, in the construction of the dream worlds of King Ludwig II of Bavaria. Making plans for this project commenced in 1868. Ludwig II purchased the Chiemsee island of Herrenwörth in 1873 as construction site, after the originally selected location in the Graswangtal near Ettal turned out to be too small. Instead of a copy of Versailles, Schloss Linderhof developed there from an additional building.

It was not the intention of Ludwig II, to copy Versailles in detail. The central rooms in the middle section of the palace – of special significance here the imposing show bedroom and the hall of mirrors – sufficed for his slipping into the role of Roi du Soleil. With regard to the gardens planned by the court gardens director Carl von Effner from 1875 onwards, this meant that merely the garden area of the central axis had to be copied in detail. This included the "parterre d´eau" towards the west, consisting of two large basins with the surmounted statues of Fama and Fortuna expressly requested by Ludwig II to highlight the mythological effect, the flower parterre with the Latona fountain and the 'Grand Canal', in front of whose mirror surface an Apollo fountain was to rise up. Visible from the bedroom, was the access avenue of 900 metres pro-

i Schloss- und Gartenverwaltung Herrenchiemsee (Palace, Castle and Gardens Administration) 83209 Herrenchiemsee
Tel. 0 80 51 / 68 87-0
Fax 0 80 51 / 68 87-99
Info-phone: 0 80 51 / 68 87-91
sgvherrenchiemsee@ bsv.bayern.de
www.herren-chiemsee.de

Size of the grounds: 42 ha

☉ Park open throughout the year

♿ No restrictions

✕

🅿 On the mainland

DB

Parterre and new palace

BAYERISCHE VERWALTUNG DER STAATLICHEN SCHLÖSSER, GÄRTEN UND SEEN

Parterre with Fama and Fortuna fountain

jected length in an easterly direction, at the lakeside end of which a boat landing stage was planned.

After extensive preparatory work shifting earth, work on the gardens could be started in 1882 – four years after laying the palace foundation stone in May 1878. The design of the garden's central axis, so important for the Herrenchiemsee experience – which constituted about one third of the total planned garden – was carried out under great pressure and largely completed by the time King Ludwig II died in June 1886. Only the Apollo fountain and the boat landing stage remained uncompleted.

View of the island called Fraueninsel

Landscape garden of the artist's house Gasteiger

Eduard-Thöny-Straße 43
86919 Holzhausen
Tel. 0 88 06/ 26 82

ⓘ Bayerische Schlösser-
verwaltung/Außenstelle
Ammersee
(Bavarian Palace and
Castle Administration/
Ammersee Branch)
Landsberger Strasse 81
82266 Inning/Stegen
Tel. 0 81 43/93 04-0
Fax 0 81 43/93 04-30
seeverwaltung.
ammersee@bsv.bayern.de

Size of the grounds: 2.0 ha

☉ Park grounds freely
accessible during the day
Guided tours of the park
on request

♿ no restrictions

🅿

A great number of artists from Munich settled on the west bank of the Ammersee around 1900. The artist's home or "Künstlerhaus" Gasteiger, built 1902–13, including residence and park, is particularly worth seeing, being considered a unique ensemble of the "Jugendstil" or art nouveau style, of Munich. The sculptor Mathias Gasteiger from Munich lived here once, together with his wife Anna Sophie, who was a painter. The gardens immediately surrounding the villa are of very formal design. The sumptuous abundance of flowers in the country garden so typical of that time, provided subjects for the flower still life painting of the lady of the house. The remaining part of the property is landscaped. In summer the garden provided a stage for the free and easy life customary among artists in those days. Mathias Gasteiger used the park as an extension of his studio, incorporating it as background to his sculpturing work. Most of the garden has been restored to its original design, after several years of successful reconstruction efforts. Today, the artist's house serves as a museum.

*Künstlerhaus (artist's house)
with gardens*

Palace Gardens Linderhof

When King Ludwig II bought the property 268 days' labour in size, around the Linderhof in the Graswangtal near Oberammergau in the year 1868, he actually intended to realise his "Bavarian Versailles" there. It became apparent in the course of development of the plans, that the dimensions of this mountainous terrain were too small for the extensive palace and garden grounds.

Thus an additional building to those palace and garden grounds emerged, as represented by the Linderhof today. As a kind of forepost for observing developments of his Versailles project, Ludwig II had a small hunting chalet next to the Linderhof grounds – the so-called Königshäuschen, or King's cottage – enlarged by three rooms for greater comfort in 1869. Two small flower parterres to the east and west of the extensions made up the decorative finish. In 1872, Ludwig II authorised his director of court gardens at the time, Carl von Effner (1831–1884) with the planning of the gardens.

The current extensions of the garden and park grounds however only took place from 1873 onwards, by which time Ludwig II had decided to realise the Versailles project on the island of Herrenchiemsee. The Königshäuschen referred to above was moved about 300 m to the west early 1874, to make space for a more uniform and extensive design. Said extension carried out in wood, remained where it was, being finished in stone to become the "Royal Villa", as the palace used to be referred to.

The gardens were simultaneously enlarged by two new sections. A large water pool with a fountain of about 25 m height was created in front of the hall of mirrors in the south wing of the building. The southern garden axis was completed by three garden terraces, crowned by a "Venus temple" and romantically enhanced by the presence of an old linden tree.

The descending terrain in front of the bedroom in the northern wing of the palace was used for the construction of a cascade comprising 30 steps. The palace was thus screened from the northern landscape by the water steps, in conjunction with the Neptune fountain from below and the so-called Music Pavilion from above.

The harsh contrast between the festive garden areas and the bordering alpine forest of firs and beeches of the Ammergau mountains was softened by a landscape park, which Effner established to encompass the regular garden grounds. In 1876, Ludwig II had two of his numerous small refuges built at the northern edge of the park: the artificial grotto illuminated in impressive colour with the help of elaborate technology and the so-called Moorish Kiosk. A hut called Hundinghütte and a Moroccan House have been rebuilt in recent times. Ludwig II had these small works of architecture originally built a few kilometres to the west of Linderhof in the middle of the Ammergau mountain forest in 1876 or 1878.

The garden and park grounds of Linderhof, with their diversity of styles and decorative features largely completed by 1877, are an exemplary demonstration of historical garden art.

ℹ Schloss- und Gartenverwaltung Linderhof (Palace, Castle and Gardens Administration) Linderhof 12 82488 Ettal Tel. 0 88 22/92 03-0 Fax 0 88 22/92 03-11 sgvlinderhof@bsv.bayern.de www.linderhof.de

Size of the grounds: 58 ha

⊘ Park grounds open throughout the year Guided tours of the park on request

♿ Restricted in some areas due to steep paths and steps

✗ – 🅿 – DB

Next double page:
Water parterre

Neptune fountain and cascade

BAYERISCHE VERWALTUNG DER STAATLICHEN SCHLÖSSER, GÄRTEN UND SEEN

English Garden Munich

i Verwaltung des Englischen
Gartens München
(Administration of the
English Garden Munich)
Englischer Garten 2
80538 München
Tel. 0 89/3 86 66 39-0
and 0 89/34 19 86
Fax 0 89/3 86 66 39-23
gvenglischergarten@
bsv.bayern.de

Size of the grounds: 374 ha

⊙ Park open throughout
the year
Guided tours of the park:
April until Oct., every third
Saturday of the month
at 2 pm (meeting point is
the Chinese Tower),
and on request

⌖ No restrictions

✕

P

DB

On 13 August 1789, the Elector Karl Theodor, impressed by the French Revolution, signed a Decree with which he expressed his sovereign intentions to restore and no longer withhold the grand hunting grounds in the Isar meadows, the Hirschanger (Stag Green) *"these most beautiful grounds of nature, from the public's hours of leisure, for the general delight of your royal capital Munich"*. On initiative of the American-born Sir Benjamin Thompson, later Imperial Count von Rumford, the laying out of military gardens had already commenced in July 1789. The electoral order was then extended to the immediate *creation of a general English garden*. For this purpose the court gardener Friedrich Ludwig Sckell of Schwetzingen was called to Munich, to start creating the first section of the gardens. Under Rumford's general supervision, numerous walking, driving and riding paths with *"bridges used as examples of various styles of building"* were created as well as a wooden Apollo temple, which was replaced by the Steinerne Bank (stone bench) in 1838. The Chinese Tower and the Chinese Inn were built in 1790, followed by the classical Rumford House one year later.

The Chinese Tower was destroyed by fire during a bombing raid in 1944. It was rebuilt in 1952 with the eager help of the citizens of Munich, as symbol of the English Garden.

The English Garden in Munich represented a completely new type of garden – the public garden. It was meant to be a public park right from the start, and according to its initiator Rumford, intended *"for the benefit of not only one segment of society, but of the entire population"*. The English Garden has been available as a recreational park for the inhabitants of Munich since 1792. During his lifetime, Rumford was honoured with a monument near the southern boundary of the English Garden in 1796. Reinhard Freiherr von Werneck succeeded Rumford in the continued development of the English Garden, who closed the military gardens in 1799, created the Kleinhesseloher Lake and enlarged the garden to the north (Hirschau). King Ludwig I had a monument erected in honour of his services in 1838, at the

Sckell monument

northern edge of the Kleinhesseloher Lake.

In 1804, Friedrich Ludwig Sckell, leading garden artist at the time, took over direction of the newly created Royal Garden Management and Artistic Directorship in Munich, and thus direct responsibility for the artistic supervision of gardening in the English Garden. After taking stock, he submitted a plan for redesign together with a memorandum to King Max I Joseph in 1807. Until his death in 1823, Sckell realised masterly design concepts in the English Garden, creating generous garden spaces, diversely interrelated views, and great variety in planting. He managed to create a landscape garden of the so-called classical phase here. A monument to commemorate Friedrich Ludwig von Sckell was erected on a tip of land in the Kleinhesseloher Lake in 1824. 1836/37 King Ludwig I finally had the Monopteros designed by Leo von Klenze built on an artificial hill. With over 370 hectares, the English Garden is one of the largest urban green spaces in the world.

Waterfall

View of the city from the Monopteros

BAYERISCHE VERWALTUNG DER STAATLICHEN SCHLÖSSER, GÄRTEN UND SEEN

Maximilian Park

i Verwaltung des Englischen
Gartens München
(Administration of the
English Garden Munich)
Englischer Garten 2
80538 München
Tel. 0 89/3 86 66 39-0
and 0 89/34 19 86
Fax 0 89/3 86 66 39-23
gvenglischergarten@
bsv.bayern.de

Size of the grounds: 30 ha

⊖ Park grounds open
throughout the year
Guided tours of the park
on request

♿ Restricted in some areas
due to steep paths and steps

By order of King Maximilian II in 1853, concrete plans were made for a promenade landscape between the villages Haidhausen and Bogenhausen, in conjunction with the Maximilianeum project. This green area was part of a master plan designed by the royal Prussian director of court gardens Peter Joseph Lenné, for the beautification of the royal capital Munich with respect to its gardens. From 1856, detail planning was taken over by Carl von Effner, a student of Lenné's. Effner remoulded the rutted high bank of the Isar, using large quantities of garden soil, into a gently undulating landscape, lined with winding paths leading through an alternation of shady woodland areas and open meadows. The terrain to the south of the Maximilianeum, the so-called Gasteig, was fashioned in a similar manner from 1861. The Luitpold Terraces were created under court garden directors Jakob Möhl and Wilhelm Zimmermann around 1890, on the highest point of which the Friedensengel (Angel of Peace) was erected between 1896 and 1899. Further monuments have been added to the park known as "Maximiliansanlagen" since 1897: 1919, the Max Ruederer fountain, 1967, a Ludwig II monument and 1982, the Father Delp stone memorial.

Luitpold terraces

Design by Wilhelm Zimmermann for the extension and rearrangement of the Maximilian Park, 1892

Photograph below: View of the Hofgarten with Diana temple

Hofgarten

The Palace Gardens (or Hofgarten) of Munich were created from 1613, outside the fortification moat of that time, simultaneous to the construction of the new residence (1611–18) under Duke Maximilian I. Centre of the previous Renaissance gardens richly furbished with round temples, mulberry walks, fountains, trellises, box ornaments and fruit trees, is the pavilion erected in 1615 by Heinrich Schön, the elder, which determines the division of the park area by cross and diagonal paths, by virtue of its eight entrance arches. The eastern, lower-lying section of the gardens, featured as an area of water until 1796. During the time that followed, the Palace Gardens were redesigned several times and adapted to current tastes. Renovation work conducted after the Second World War, was based on the original path structure and tree arrangement established from 1776 onwards.

The area preceding the residence behind the palace garden gate created by Klenze in 1816 was reinstated to its original design of 1853, according to plans by Carl Effner senior, featuring the typical plant beds characteristic of that time.

i Verwaltung der Residenz München (Administration of the Residence Munich) Residenzstraße 1 80333 München Tel. 0 89/2 90 67-1 Fax 0 89/2 90 67-2 25 ResidenzMuenchen@ bsv.bayern.de

Size of the grounds: 4.0 ha

☉ Park grounds open throughout the year Guided tours of the park on request

♿ No restrictions

✕ – DB

Nymphenburg Palace Gardens

ℹ Schloss- und Garten-
verwaltung Nymphenburg
(Palace, Castle and
Gardens Administration)
Eingang 1
80638 München
Tel. 0 89 / 1 79 08-0
Fax 0 89 / 1 79 08-6 27
sgvnymphenburg@
bsv.bayern.de

Size of the grounds: 180 ha

🕓 Park opening hours –
Main gate:
Jan. Feb.:
6.30 am to 6.00 pm
March:
6.00 am to 6.30 pm
April:
6.00 am to 8.30 pm
May – Aug.:
6.00 am to 9.30 pm
September:
6.00 am to 8.30 pm

View of the palace from the cascade

The Bavarian Elector Ferdinand Maria presented his wife Henriette Adelaide with the inn, Schwaige Kemnat, to the west of the royal capital Munich, on the occasion of the long-awaited birth of a successor to the throne Max Emanuel in 1663. The Electress created her "borgo de la ninfe" here, a summer palace with small gardens. From 1701, Max Emanuel had the palace enlarged, the gardens reshaped and a canal dug out to divert water from the Würm to the park. Max Emanuel however had to leave Bavaria, in consequence of his defeat in the Spanish War of Succession in 1704. This lead to a temporary interruption of all work.

It was only in the period from 1715 to 1726 that decisive constructional work was carried out to turn the palace and gardens into the Baroque highlight of ubiquitous fame. Nymphenburg Park was completed based on a design by Dominique Girard and the cooperation of Joseph Effner. Axial-symmetrical designed gardens with an elaborate parterre with hedged areas bordering on both sides, featuring facilities intended for the amusement of the court, were created in front of the west side of the palace. In juxtaposition to this intensively designed section of the gardens, was an extensive forest-like park, dominated by a central-axial canal and divided by numerous avenues and perspective axes. Located here in symmetrical arrangement, were also the pavilion-style park castles with their regular gardens, the Baden- and Pagodenburg, the hermitage Madgalenenklause, and the Amalienburg erected 1731–39.

In the year 1800, the Bavarian Elector Max IV Joseph commissioned the reshaping of the landscape of Nymphenburg. Unaffected by this, were only the central-axial parts of the Baroque gar-

Cascade

🕘 October:
6.00 am to 7.00 pm
November:
6.30 am to 6.00 pm
December
6.30 am to 5.30 pm
The other park gates are shut half an hour earlier!
Exhibition on the Park in the Geranium House, open from 1.4. – 30.9.:
9.00 am – 6.00 pm
Guided tours of the park: May until Oct.: every first Saturday of the month at 2.00 pm (meeting point is the Museum Shop Nymphenburg)

♿ No restrictions

Great lake and Badenburg

dens, i.e. the parterre near the palace reduced to its basic structure, the canal with the avenues on both sides and the cascade. Friedrich Ludwig von Sckell, leading garden artist of his time, carried out re-landscaping of the grounds of Nymphenburg between 1804 and 1823. He replaced the original regular systematic axes and avenues, canals, water basins, beds and hedged areas, with natural-looking design elements, a selection of trees and shrubs arranged to grow as nature intended, meadows with moulded surface levels and artfully contoured woodland borders, lakes and brooks with banks and islands shaped true to nature, and elegantly winding paths. Sckell thereby created stimulating landscape scenery, which integrated the Baroque pavilions as effectively as the classical Monopteros by the Great Lake erected in 1865, to replace two earlier wooden constructions.

In Nymphenburg, Friedrich Ludwig von Sckell succeeded in creating a classical landscape garden, whose special charm lay in the continuation of characteristic features of the gardens originating from previous and fundamentally different stylistic epochs. The grounds have remained virtually unchanged in their basic structure until today.

Lake Badenburg with Monopteros

Schleißheim Palace Gardens

The gardens of Schleißheim, with their limiting canals and the extensive bosket area between Lustheim and the Old Palace were conceived by Enrico Zuccalli, in connection with the erection of the palace, Schloss Lustheim, from 1684. A comprehensive canal system was created from 1689, as prerequisite for a Baroque pleasure ground of style and grandeur. On this basis, Dominique Girard, who was simultaneously active in Nymphenburg, looked after the creation of the gardens in parallel to construction of the New Palace in the period between 1717 and 1726. A sunken parterre with exten-sive decorative beds, sculptures and a spectacular cascade were established in front of the New Palace. The central axis, being the garden's absolute principle of order, initially served as alley for the game of maille, which was popular at court, before being converted to a canal at the end of the 18th century. The bosket area was equipped with fountain arrangements, small architecture and amusement facilities.

The circular buildings originally arranged in a semi-circle in the background of Schloss Lustheim, serving as orangery, soon dilapidated, having been replaced

i Schloss- und Gartenver-waltung Schleißheim (Palace, Castle and Gardens Administration) Max-Emanuel-Platz 1 85764 Oberschleißheim Tel. 0 89/31 58 72-0 Fax 0 89/31 58 72-50 sgvschleissheim@ bsv.bayern.de

Size of the grounds: 95 ha

⊘ Daily from 8.00 am, Jan. & Feb., Nov. & Dec. until 5.00 pm March and October until 6.00 pm April and September until 7.00 pm May until August until 8.00 pm Guided tours of the park on request

♿ No restrictions

✕ – **P** – **DB**

BAVARIA

View of the New Palace from Schloss Lustheim

by hedges today. The avenues emanating radially from Lustheim are directed towards landmarks in the landscape.

Even though the gardens were neglected at the start of the 19th century, no reshaping of the landscape took place and the gardens were therefore not essentially changed, in contrast to the fate of many Baroque gardens in those days. Schleißheim is therefore one of the very few Baroque gardens, which have retained their original layout.

By order of King Ludwig I, Carl Effner restored the gardens from 1865–68, maintaining the old structure, but adding ornamental shapes typical of that time, most of which were lost again during the Second World War. The design of the park between the Old and New Palace is also accredited to Carl Effner.

Lustheim Palace from the east

Side avenue

Flowers in the parterre

BAYERISCHE VERWALTUNG DER STAATLICHEN SCHLÖSSER, GÄRTEN UND SEEN

Hofgarten 1
97209 Veitshöchstheim
Tel. 09 31/9 15 82

i Schloss- und Garten-
verwaltung Würzburg
(Palace, Castle and
Gardens Administration)
Residenzplatz 2, Tor B
97070 Würzburg
Tel. 09 31/3 55 17-0
Fax 09 31/5 19 25
sgvwuerzburg@
bsv.bayern.de

Size of the grounds: 12 ha

⊘ Palace gardens open
throughout the year from
7.00 am until dusk or
8.00 pm at the latest
Guided tours of the park
on request

♿ No restrictions

✕

P

DB

Veitshöchstheim Palace Gardens

Veitshöchheim is primarily famous for its beautiful Rococo gardens. Prince Bishop Johann Phillip von Greiffenclau had already started the transformation of the old game reserve into a decorative and pleasure garden, by construction of the main paths, terraces and lakes from 1702 onwards. The gardens were only slightly modified during the first half of the 18th century, causing the great garden enthusiast Prince Bishop Adam Friedrich von Seinsheim (ruled 1755–1779), to order a final extensive redesign in-detail, which was largely completed by the time of his death in 1779. To this day, Veitshöchheim Palace Gardens have retained much of the abundance of style, form and beauty created under Seinsheim, by the designing court gardeners Georg Joseph Oth (until 1777) and Johann Anton Oth (from 1777). More than 300 stone benches and sculptures by the court sculptors Johann Wolfgang van der Auvera (died 1756), Ferdinand Tietz (1708–1777) and Johann Peter Wagner (1730–1809) from Würzburg, populate the approximately 11.9 ha of park area. They represent animals, mythological creatures, the court society and personifications of the gods and the arts.

Kilometres of hedgerow walls divide the gardens into many small rooms, some of which house fruit trees or even small fountains. Shaped and naturally growing avenues of deciduous and coniferous trees with cleverly arranged view axes, run throughout the entire gardens. Situated in the south-eastern corner of the gardens, is the snail house or Schneckenhaus, with its mythological creatures fashioned from shells and coloured stones. The hedge theatre or Heckentheater, is located in the neighbouring "maze" area. A short distance from there, two dainty sandstone pavilions with pillars reminiscent of palm trees and roofs decorated with pineapples invite to linger. Shady hornbeam walks alternate with light-filled cabinets in the adjacent "pergola walk area". The stroller finally reaches the "lake area" with the small and large lakes. The latter contains an artificial mountain background, with a Pegasus rising from its peak. The old water tower, whose reservoir originally fed the waterworks of the large lake, is an important component of the complex

*Water spewing ram
in the northern hedge cabinet*

irrigation and drainage system running through the entire gardens. The copper beeches, plane trees and weeping willows, which have grown into mighty picturesque trees, were planted in the 19th century. They were intended to relieve from the garden's austere geometrical shapes that were felt to be too monotonous in those days. Today those very trees as well as the oldest design elements are integral components of these unique monumental gardens.

The sale of the northern section of the gardens in 1969 must be considered as a regrettable discrepancy in the otherwise continuous history of the park. New planting of numerous fruit trees since 1994 in the hedged areas, and the cultivation of seasoning herbs and old varieties of vegetables since 1994 in the location of the previous kitchen garden, has resulted in the re-emergence of an intricate combination of decorative and useful gardening elements so typical of Veitshöchheim Palace Gardens.

Great lake with Parnassus

View to the north from the grotto house

BAYERISCHE VERWALTUNG DER STAATLICHEN SCHLÖSSER, GÄRTEN UND SEEN

i Schloss- und Garten-
verwaltung Würzburg
(Palace, Castle and
Gardens Administration)
Residenzplatz 2, Tor B
97070 Würzburg
Tel. 09 31/3 55 17-0
Fax 09 31/5 19 25
sgvwuerzburg@
bsv.bayern.de

**Unesco World
Cultural Heritage**

Size of the grounds: 9.3 ha

⊘ Palace gardens open
throughout the year from
7.00 am until dusk or
8.00 pm at the latest
Guided tours of the park
on request

♿ Restricted in some areas
due to steep paths and steps

✕

P

DB

Würzburg Palace Gardens

On completion of construction work on the residence, the final development of Würzburg Palace Gardens or the Hofgarten was tackled during the rule of the Prince Bishop of Würzburg, Adam Friedrich von Seinsheim (ruled 1755–1779). Seinsheim employed the Bohemian-born garden artist Johann Prokop Mayer (1735–1804) as new court gardener to help him in the realisation of the project. Mayer skilfully divided the awkwardly sized garden terrain rising steeply towards the bastions, into individual, symmetrical self-contained sections. This resulted in the creation of approximately three equal sized parts, namely the East Garden, the South Garden and the nursery grounds. Mayer filled all sections of the gardens with an abundance of topiary fruit trees, hedges, trellises, potted plants and pergola walks. He developed the area referred to as the East Garden by extending the central mid-axis of the residence. This commenced with a large circular broderie parterre. It was intended to build

a cascade into the area rising up to the bastion behind. This was however never realised. In contrast to the East Garden, the South Garden lies on a plane area. Today, this part of the gardens is characterised by eight large yews standing centrally around a circular water basin and trimmed to perfect cones. The decorative figures around the Hofgarten originate from the workshop of the court sculptor Johann Peter Wagner. Famous are also the elaborate wrought-iron garden gates, manufactured in the workshop of the court metalworker Johann Georg Oegg.

In the past few years, the flower borders of the East and South Gardens have been planted with inspiration from historical designs, and new fruit trees, which are to be cultivated according to old training methods, have been planted in the restored kitchen gardens below the orangery in 2001. A small 19th century landscape presents itself beyond the formal parts of the gardens towards the city.

*Design by Johann Prokop Mayer
of the East Garden*

East Garden

South Garden

BAYERISCHE VERWALTUNG DER STAATLICHEN SCHLÖSSER, GÄRTEN UND SEEN

Castle slopes and grounds of the Burg Burghausen
Burg Nr. 48
84489 Burghausen

ℹ Burgverwaltung Landshut
(Castle Administration)
Burg Trausnitz 168
84036 Landshut
Tel. 08 71 / 9 24 11-0
Fax 08 71 / 9 24 11-40

Castle grounds of Cadolzburg
90556 Cadolzburg

ℹ Burgverwaltung Nürnberg
(Castle Administration)
Auf der Burg 13
90403 Nürnberg
Tel. 09 11 / 22 57 26
Fax 09 11 / 2 05 91 17

Grounds of Schloss Ehrenburg

ℹ Schloss- und Gartenverwaltung Coburg
(Palace, Castle and Gardens Administration)
Schloss Ehrenburg
96450 Coburg
Tel. 09561 / 80 88-0, Fax 80 88-40

Palace Gardens, Hofgarten Ellingen
91792 Ellingen
Tel. 09 141 / 9 74 79-0
Fax 09 141 / 9 74 79-7

ℹ Schloss- und Gartenverwaltung Ansbach
(Palace, Castle and Gardens Administration)
Promenade 27
91522 Ansbach
Tel. 09 81 / 95 38 39-0
Fax 09 81 / 95 38 39-40

Lawn areas of the Fraueninsel
83256 Frauenchiemsee
Tel. 0 80 54 / 9 07-0

ℹ Schloss- und Gartenverwaltung
(Palace, Castle and Gardens Administration)
Herrenchiemsee
83209 Herrenchiemsee
Tel. 0 80 51 / 68 87-0
Fax 0 80 51 / 68 87-99

Grounds of "Königshaus Schachen"
82467 Garmisch-Partenkirchen

ℹ Schloss- und Gartenverwaltung Linderhof
(Palace, Castle and Gardens Administration)
Linderhof 12
82488 Ettal
Tel. 0 88 22 / 92 03-0
Fax 0 88 22 / 92 03-11

Palace Gardens, Schlossgarten Höchstädt
Herzogin-Anna-Straße 52
89420 Höchstädt an der Donau

ℹ Schlossverwaltung Neuburg
(Palace and Castle Administration)
Residenzstraße 2
86633 Neuburg
Tel. 0 84 31 / 88 97
Fax 0 84 31 / 42 68 9

Grounds of the Hall of Liberty, Befreiungshalle
in Kelheim
Befreiungshallestraße
93309 Kelheim

ℹ Verwaltung der Befreiungshalle Kelheim
Befreiungshallestraße 3
93309 Kelheim
Tel. 0 94 41 / 6 82 07-0
Fax 0 94 41 / 6 82 07-7

Castle slopes and grounds
of the Plassenburg in Kulmbach
95326 Kulmbach
Tel. 0 92 21 / 82 20-0
Fax 0 92 21 / 82 20-26

ℹ Schloss- und Gartenverwaltung
(Palace, Castle and Gardens Administration)
Bayreuth-Eremitage
Ludwigstr. 21
95444 Bayreuth
Tel. 09 21 / 7 59 69-0
Fax 09 21 / 7 59 69-15

Castle slopes and grounds of Burg Trausnitz
84036 Landshut

ℹ Burgverwaltung Landshut
(Castle Administration)
Burg Trausnitz 168
84036 Landshut
Tel. 08 71 / 9 24 11-0
Fax 08 71 / 9 24 11-40

Castle slopes and grounds of Burg Lauenstein
Burgstraße 3
96337 Ludwigsstadt
Tel. 0 92 63 / 4 00
Fax 0 92 63 / 97 44 22

ℹ Schloss- und Gartenverwaltung
(Palace, Castle and Gardens Administration)
Bamberg
Domplatz 8
96049 Bamberg
Tel. 09 51 / 5 19 39-0
oder 09 51 / 5 19 39-1 14
Fax 05 91 / 5 19 39-1 29

Grounds surrounding the Bavaria statue
Theresienhöhe 16
80339 München

ℹ Verwaltung des Englischen Gartens München
(Administration of the English Garden
Munich)
Englischer Garten 2
80538 München
Tel. 0 89 / 3 86 66 39-0 und 0 89 / 34 19 86
Fax 0 89 / 3 86 66 39-23

Palace Gardens, Schlossgarten Neuburg
Residenzstraße 2
86633 Neuburg

ℹ Schlossverwaltung Neuburg
(Palace and Castle Administration)
Residenzstraße 2
86633 Neuburg
Tel. 0 84 31 / 88 97
Fax 0 84 31 / 42 68 9

Castle Gardens, Burggarten Nürnberg
Auf der Burg 13
90403 Nürnberg

ℹ Burgverwaltung Nürnberg
(Castle Administration)
Auf der Burg 13
90403 Nürnberg
Tel. 09 11 / 22 57 26, Fax 09 11 / 2 05 91 17

Castle grounds of Burg Prunn in the Altmühltal
93339 Riedenburg

ℹ Verwaltung der Befreiungshalle Kelheim
(Administration)
Befreiungshallestraße 3
93309 Kelheim
Tel. 0 94 41 / 6 82 07-0, Fax 0 94 41 / 6 82 07-7

Castle grounds of the Rosenburg in Riedenburg
93339 Riedenburg
Tel. 0 94 42 / 27 52
Fax 0 94 42 / 32 87

ℹ Verwaltung der Befreiungshalle Kelheim
(Administration)
Befreiungshallestraße 3
93309 Kelheim
Tel. 0 94 41 / 6 82 07-0, Fax 0 94 41 / 6 82 07-7

Castle grounds and forest slopes
of Schloss Neuschwanstein
Neuschwansteinstraße 20
87645 Schwangau

ℹ Schlossverwaltung Neuschwanstein
(Castle Administration)
Neuschwansteinstraße 20
87654 Schwangau
Tel. 0 83 62 / 8 10 35

Gardens of the artist's home, Künstlerhaus Exter
Übersee am Chiemsee
Blumenweg 5
83236 Übersee-Feldwies
Tel. 0 86 42 / 89 50-83, Fax 0 86 42 / 89 50-85

ℹ Schloss- und Gartenverwaltung
(Palace, Castle and Gardens Administration)
Herrenchiemsee
83209 Herrenchiemsee
Tel. 0 80 51 / 68 87-0, Fax 0 80 51 / 68 87-99

Grounds of the old villa: Alte Villa in
Holzhausen/Ammersee

ℹ Bayerische Schlösserverwaltung/
Außenstelle Ammersee
(Bavarian Palace and Castle
Administration/Ammersee Branch)
Landsberger Straße 81
82266 Inning/Stegen
Tel. 0 81 43 / 93 04-0, Fax 0 81 43 / 93 04-30

Grounds, castle slopes and princely gardens
of the fortress, Festung Marienberg
97082 Würzburg

ℹ Schloss- und Gartenverwaltung Würzburg
(Palace, Castle and Gardens Administration)
Residenzplatz 2, Tor B
97070 Würzburg
Tel. 09 31 / 3 55 17-0, Fax 09 31 / 5 19 25

Berlin
Brandenburg

STIFTUNG PREUSSISCHE SCHLÖSSER
UND GÄRTEN
BERLIN-BRANDENBURG

BERLIN-BRANDENBURG FOUNDATION
OF PRUSSIAN STATELY HOMES AND
GARDENS

STIFTUNG PREUSSISCHE SCHLÖSSER UND GÄRTEN BERLIN-BRANDENBURG

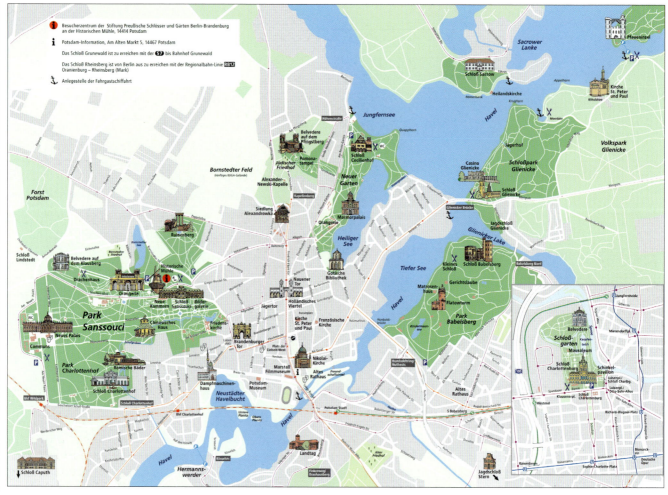

The gardens in and around Potsdam

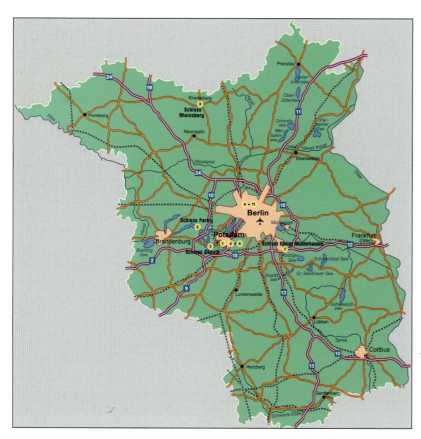

Brandenburg and Berlin

Potsdam and Brandenburg

◁ *The Victoria on the terrace in front of the orangery palace in Sanssouci Park*

Potsdam, New Gardens – Heiliger See (Holy Lake) with red and green house

THE GARDENS OF THE BERLIN-BRANDENBURG FOUNDATION OF PRUSSIAN STATELY HOMES AND GARDENS

The modest creations bearing witness to the garden art of Brandenburg up to that time fell victim to the ravages of the Thirty Year War. This meant that the creation of the first permanent demonstration of Brandenburg-Prussian garden art was reserved for the great Elector (born in 1626, 1640–1688). He was a passionate and determined promoter of gardens and regional culture. The pleasure grounds of the city palaces of Berlin and Potsdam were redesigned in accordance with Dutch ideals, and new gardens were established in Oranienburg and Köpenick, as well as in the area around Potsdam – in Bornim, Caputh and Glienicke. North Germany's first garden in the style of André Le Nôtre was created from 1696 onwards by Simeon Godeau, a student of Le Nôtres: the later first Prussian queen Sophie Charlotte (born in 1668, 1688-1705). As crown prince, Friedrich the Great (born in 1712, 1740–1786), created the beginnings of the gardens of Rheinsberg, commencing in 1744 with the establishment of the gardens of Sanssouci in Potsdam, which was to become his second residence. Potsdam henceforth developed as centre of Prussian garden art. From 1787 onwards, King Friedrich Wilhelm II had the landscape-style New Gardens created on the banks of the Heiligen See (Holy Lake), based on Wörlitz as a model. This heralded the beginning of garden art practised in the water landscape of Potsdam. Design of the Pfaueninsel (Peacock Island) ensued in 1793. Although the court gardeners were under immediate direction of King Friedrich II, his successor established a special garden administration, headed by a director of gardens from 1798. The park landscape of Potsdam owes its existence to a fortunate cooperation of the ingenious garden artist and organiser Peter Joseph Lenné (1789–1866), who commenced his 50 years of activity in Potsdam in 1816, with the great architect Karl Friedrich Schinkel (1781–1841) and the crown prince and King Friedrich Wilhelm IV (born in 1795, 1840–1861). New gardens were created in Glienicke, Charlottenhof and Babelsberg, and the chain of lakes known as Havel, became the centre of this garden kingdom. The influence of Prince Hermann von Pückler-Muskau (1785–1871) in Park Babelsberg, lead to further heights. At the end of the monarchy, the majority of the former royal palace and garden grounds of Prussia came under the care of the administration of state palaces, castles and gardens, founded 1 April 1927. The dissolution of Prussia in 1945 resulted in the demise of this administration. The stately homes formerly under its care were divided up among the relevant occupying nations. Two sections of the central territory of the old Prussian administration of palaces, castles and gardens survived separated by the East-West German state border, in Potsdam and West Berlin. After the reunification of Germany in 1990, these joined together as the Berlin-Brandenburg Foundation of Prussian Stately Homes and Gardens (SPSG) by state agreement reached between the Federal Government and the Lands of Berlin and Brandenburg. This preserves, studies and restores the 13 historical gardens of a total area of 709 ha in Potsdam, Berlin and the Mark of Brandenburg. The stately homes and parks of Potsdam and Berlin were added to the World Cultural Heritage List in 1990. The central task of the garden directorate over the past years has been the healing of wounds inflicted by the Wall put up right across the park landscape of Potsdam-Berlin.

i Visitor centre
Tel. 03 31/96 94 200/201,
Fax 03 31/96 94 107

Size: approx. 30 ha

☉ The gardens are freely
accessible daily throughout
the year from dawn to dusk

✕

P Near the historical mill,
beyond the Luisenplatz

🚌

Sanssouci Park – Lustgarten (Pleasure Ground)

King Friedrich II chose a hill known as the "Wüsten Berg" (Desert Hill) in the north west of the town of Potsdam for the construction of his summer residence. The individual creation began in 1744 with the construction of six vineyard terraces, arching inwards centrally, for the cultivation of fruit, followed by the construction of a crowning summer residence by Georg Wenzeslaus von Knobelsdorff in 1745. A Baroque parterre with four broderie sections and four sunken areas of lawn lay at the foot of the terraces split up by yew tree pyramids and potted orange trees. Five rows of chestnuts lined both vineyard and parterre. The central axis continued on the other side of the park ditch with four avenue rows along two narrow ditches, on either side of which gardener's cottages were built in 1751/52.

The gardens were however developed along a principal avenue of almost 2 km, from the obelisk erected in 1748 in the east of the pleasure ground, up to a grotto started in 1751 at the western end of the Rehgarten (Deer Gardens), parallel to a hilly range.

To the east of the Sanssouci terraces, below a large greenhouse built in 1747 – having been replaced by a painting gallery by Johann Gottfried Büring during 1753 to 1755 – and a Neptune grotto built from 1751 to 1757, areas divided regularly by paths, surrounded by high hedges and originally intended for the cultivation of fruit, bordered both sides of the principal avenue.

To the west of the Sanssouci terraces, below the orangery built in 1747, which was converted to the Neue Kammern (New Chambers) by Georg Christian Unger between 1771 and 1774, lay a parterre with cherry trees planted in orderly rows. A bosket lined with high hedges featuring circular flowerbeds and symmetrically arranged paths, is situated on either side of the principal avenue.

The principal avenue of Sanssouci Park leading towards the New Palais, with the small fountain in the "Oranierrondell" in the foreground

The Baroque parterre and the terraces in front of Sanssouci palace

Sanssouci Park – Rehgarten/Ruinenberg/Klausberg

The Rehgarten (Deer Gardens) characterised by ancient forest segments and originally enclosed, is adjacent to the western side of the Pleasure Ground. A richly decorated marble colonnade was built on the main avenue by Knobelsdorff in 1751/52, located roughly in the centre of the park, which was not intended for hunting. Densely planted English avenues meandered along the sides, opening up to garden salons and allowing a very limited view. Individual gardens were also established in the vicinity around the Chinese House built by Büring from about 1754 to 1756, with small parterres, winding paths, a zig-zag shaped pergola walk and several walls for fruit cultivation in a dense bosket area. At the end of the main avenue, Friedrich II had the New Palais erected between 1763 and 1769 by Büring and Carl Philipp von Gontard, in place of

a commenced grotto, with a semi-circular lawn parterre at its front designed by Heinrich Christian Eckstein. The two "communs" linked with a semi-circular triumphal arch behind the large palace building, completed the regularly designed garden area with its sunken lawn squares.

Near the vineyard, with its three talut walls to the north of a mulberry avenue, outside the gardens of Frederick the Great, Gontard built a Drachenhaus (Dragon House) in the shape of a pagoda, as dwelling for the winegrower, and Unger built a Belvedere on the Klausberg from 1770 to 1772.

From 1786, Friedrich Wilhelm II had the Baroque parterres in the Pleasure Ground and the large sections in the Rehgarten reshaped in a natural-sentimental style by Johann August Eyserbeck the younger. The ditches in the gardens themselves

ℹ Visitor centre
Tel. 03 31/96 94 200/201,
Fax 03 31/96 94 107

Size: approx. 190 ha

⊙ The gardens are freely accessible daily throughout the year from dawn to dusk

✕

🅿 Parking facilities near the New Palais

🚌

were dug out further to form long ponds with wave-shaped banks, numerous winding paths were added and cross views were hewn out. The colonnade on the main avenue was pulled down in 1797. From 1821, the entire landscape of the Rehgarten was gradually redesigned under Peter Joseph Lenné, with exception of the Baroque main avenue, which was retained. The water ditches were filled in with earth around 1880.

To the north of Palace Sanssouci in 1748, Friedrich II had a large round water reservoir created on a hill approximately 600 m away, for the fountains being planned. This hill became known as the Ruinenberg (Ruin Hill) on account

of the artificial ruins that were built on it.

It was however only under Friedrich IV that a steam-powered pump house in the shape of a mosque constructed in the Havel bay in Neustadt by Friedrich Ludwig Persius in 1842, made it possible to feed the greatly increased number of fountains and irrigate the plants, by means of an extensive pipe system via the elevated storage tank on the Ruinenberg. At the same time, Lenné took in hand the entire landscaping of the Ruinenberg, with elegantly winding footpaths and carriageways and plenty of good views of the countryside.

The Sicilian Gardens were established north-west of the palace from 1856 with a

Fountain called "Rossebrunnen" and cascade as seen from the court of honour of Sanssouci Palace towards ruin hill

luxurious abundance of southern plants, and as their counterpart, the Nordic Gardens characterised by their regular shapes being maintained until 1860, on the other side of the mulberry avenue. The Orangery Palace was built by Friedrich August Stüler and Ludwig Ferdinand Hesse on the Bornstedter Höhe (Bornstedt Heights) between 1851 and 1860. Lenné created landscape gardens in the north, with generous planting provided for the three regularly designed terraces in the south of the long building. Under Wilhelm II, landscape gardens were created from 1902 to 1907 by Georg Potente and named after him, located between the Orangery Palace and the Belvedere on the Klausberg, on either side of a connecting avenue of four rows of trees.

Sicilian garden with Medici vase, pergola walk and sea lion fountain on the supporting wall towards the mulberry avenue

Sanssouci Park – Marlygarten

i Visitor centre
Tel. 03 31/96 94 200/201,
Fax 03 31/96 94 107

Size: approx. 3 ha

☉ The gardens are freely
accessible daily throughout
the year from dawn to dusk

✳

P Beyond Luisenplatz

🚌

The Marlygarten was established as a kitchen garden in 1715 by the Soldier King, and named specifically to ridicule the Sun King's luxurious Marly-le-Roy. When Friedrich Wilhelm IV began construction of the Friedenskirche (Church of Peace) at the edge of these kitchen gardens, 100 years after laying the foundation stone for a churchless Sanssouci, Lenné saw an opportunity present itself for creating "a pearl among landscape gardens" out of the flat vegetable patch right in front of his service apartment. The kitchen garden wall, which separated the now purposely preserved and restored hedge quarters of Frederick the Great's pleasure ground from the new landscape garden, was retained. Old and new was deliberately juxtaposed. Deep philosophical-religious symbolism was behind this, of which the Marlygarten is filled in every detail. By virtue of using the narrow side paths, the Marlygarten with its mere 200 x 120 m, its artfully contoured delicate surfaces, and its nearing and receding woody landscape backgrounds, displays a spatial diversity making it appear at least as wide as it is long.

View from the front churchyard of the Friedenskirche through the Marlygarten towards the blue-white column

Flora hill with Lennésque flower beds in the Marlygarten

The pond called Friedensteich ("Frieden" meaning peace) near the arcade leading to the Friedenskirche

Sanssouci Park – Charlottenhof

i   Visitor centre
Tel. 03 31 / 96 94 200/201,
Fax 03 31 / 96 94 107

Size: approx. 70 ha

⊙   The gardens are freely
accessible daily throughout
the year from dawn to dusk

✕

P   Parking facilities near
the New Palais

🚌

Park Charlottenhof bordering on Park Sanssouci in the south is Lenné's most subtle creation, which he commenced in 1825, in cooperation with the architect Karl Friedrich Schinkel and the commissioning Crown Prince Friedrich Wilhelm. The terrain he had to work with was as flat as a table, and so he had to create everything from scratch, including ground contouring, water surfaces and groups of trees and shrubs, in harmony with the network of paths. Schinkel had instructions to simultaneously transform the existing manor house to a Roman villa for the Crown Prince. Architect and gardener developed an east-west orientated geometrically arranged architectural and garden axis. Earth excavations for achieving the picturesque contours of the Maschinenteich (Machine Pond) were accompanied by ornamental structuring of the plain extending towards the north with 8 ground elevations and extensive design using groups of trees and shrubs. The architectonic-garden axis began at the machine pond with a steam engine house set up as vantage point – unfortunately removed in 1923 – running through a rose garden, terrace, palace, a dark poet's grove, up to a hippodrome hidden in the woods. This axis not only represents a rebirth of Greek-Roman ideals but is at the same time an illustration of human history and the indi-

Deciduous shrubs in front of the Albanian-style lattice-work fence of the court gardener's cottage front garden and the Roman baths in Park Charlottenhof

viduality of human life, with views directed from east to west: of Roman baths, vineyard and the cupola of the New Palais. Lenné distributed islands of dense, grove-like groups of trees and shrubs over the wide plain in the north of the Rehgarten in such a manner that the visitor following the wide curves of the paths, is alternately presented with opening and closing perspectives of inter-merging spaces and glimpses beyond. Strategically planted groups of bushes make the severe geometry of the archi-tectonic-garden axis virtually invisible, allowing only picturesque partial views of individual elements. All the more pronounced and surprising is the effect of the geometry of architecture and gardens.

View of the rose gardens from the pergola steps of Palace Charlottenhof

View form the garden terrace by the Roman baths over the machine pond towards Palace Charlottenhof

Lindstedt

i Visitor centre
Tel. 03 31/96 94 200/201,
Fax 03 31/96 94 107

Size: approx. 2.2 ha

⊘ The gardens are freely
accessible daily throughout
the year from dawn to dusk

✕

🅿 Near the palace gardens
in the Lindstedter Chaussee
(Linstedt high road)

Lindstedt Palace Gardens lie north west of the New Palais near woods called Katharienenholz. The property acquired in 1828 by Friedrich Wilhelm IV was converted to a villa in imitation of classical forms by Hesse in 1859, a regular garden being established on the long shape of the 2.2 ha of land by Lenné in 1861. Secluded and with but few views of the beautified landscape towards the village Eiche, bench-lined paths lead to shady pergola walks and exedra-like resting points. Allotment gardens have been located in the northern section of the park since 1954.

Paretz

i Visitor centre
Tel. 03 31/96 94 200/201,
Fax 03 31/96 94 107

Size: approx. 7.2 ha

⊘ The gardens are freely
accessible daily throughout
the year from dawn to dusk

✕

🅿 Near the Kirchgarten
(Church Garden)

There is no information regarding any gardens situated in Paretz, north of the island of Potsdam prior to 1800. The property was purchased as early 1797 as summer residence for the Crown Prince couple Friedrich Wilhelm III and Luise. Immediately after that, David Gilly was commissioned to redesign palace and village, and the court gardener David Garmatter, to design the park. Hofmarschall (lord chamberlain), Valentin von Massow directed and organised the enterprise, his place of residence Steinhöfel being taken as a model for many design aspects. The palace was ready to move into by the following year and the basic layout of the gardens could already be experienced. Completion of the village grounds took until about 1804 and was to become a prime example of the art of Prussian agricultural methods, from an aesthetic and commercial point of view. The early landscape style of garden design typical of that time, with numerous sentimental small architectural objects placed in dominant locations, unites the entire grounds. The grounds are constituted of three components of differing character: south of the palace, up to the ditch known as Kettengraben, are the Palace Gardens previously reserved for the ruling classes, in the central triangle between palace, church and Gothic forge, the Kirchgarten (Church Gardens) as a very refined form of village green, and finally to the west on a ridge of hills the Rohrhausgarten, named after a very picturesque rustic pavilion with an excellent view.

Being more or less maintained until the end of the 19th century, a phase of dilapidation ensued particularly with regard to the park staffages. When a farming college moved into the palace after the Second World War, it was changed beyond recognition. Blocks of flats built in the 1960's enclosed the Rohrhausgarten and preservation work on the historical gardens began with the Church Gardens 20 years later. Reconstruction of the palace and foregrounds commenced in 1999, being handed over in conjunction with an exhibition three years later. Restoration of the other gardens will take much longer, but the old trees, earth contouring, paths and buildings already convey a good impression of the former glory of this charming ensemble today.

Caputh

i Visitor centre
Tel. 03 31/96 94 200/201,
Fax 03 31/96 94 107

Size: approx. 3.4 ha

⊘ The gardens are freely
accessible daily throughout
the year from dawn to dusk

✕

🅿 Follow directions
for parking in the area

Caputh lies south west of Potsdam behind a lake called Templiner See. Electress Katharina already had a summer residence there in the 16th century, which included an exemplary farm estate comprising vineyard, ponds, a manor and palace gardens. In 1662, the Electoral Quartermaster Philipp de Chieze rebuilt the palace destroyed during the Thirty Year War, with terraced Baroque gardens. After his death, it became part of the electoral estates circling Potsdam, was decorated further still and used mainly for celebrations and hunting parties until 1713. After a century of leasing and commercial utilisation followed its sale to Lieutenant General von Thümen. The latter had the garden landscape reshaped from 1820 based on an improvement plan by Lenné, and added a Kavalierhaus between palace and Havel. The introduction of small utility areas after 1908 hardly changed the arrangement of the gardens. Various schools moved into the palace after the Second World War, and the garden suffered neglect. Its transfer to the Heritage Trust in 1994 heralded the restoration of the gardens, accompanied by archaeological digging for Baroque remnants. Since the opening of the palace in 1999, the gardens may also be appreciated again.

The landscape gardens designed by Lenné near the Baroque Palace Caputh

STIFTUNG PREUSSISCHE SCHLÖSSER UND GÄRTEN BERLIN-BRANDENBURG

Neuer Garten (New Gardens) and Pfingstberg (Whitsun Hill)

i Visitor centre
Tel. 03 31/96 94 200/201,
Fax 03 31/96 94 107

Size: approx. 93 ha

⊙ The gardens are freely
accessible daily throughout
the year from dawn to dusk

✕

P Close to Palace Cecilienhof

🚌

The New Gardens lie exactly in the middle of the World Heritage Region represented by the garden landscape of Potsdam. Its story began with the purchase of a central piece of land by Crown Prince Friedrich Wilhelm II. He took over without modifications, the former vineyard area including the house. In the year 1787, one year after commencing his reign, design of the New Gardens began, the name being part of the programmatic rejection of the old Baroque Park Sanssouci. Johann August Eyserbeck was appointed as artistic director. As son and student of the court gardener Johann Friedrich Eyserbeck from Wörlitz, he was able to guarantee the realisation of Friedrich Wilhelm's ideal, based on English gardens, in contrast to the court gardeners of Potsdam. Unfavourable for the uniform character of the sentimental gardens was the process of acquistion of the plots of land over several years. Important new buildings were established between 1787 and 1792, in addition to the incorporation of former dwelling houses: marble palais, kitchen in the form of a Roman temple ruin, shingle house, orangery, grotto, dairy, ice cellar in pyramid shape and the Dutch etablissement. A representative example of Prussian highway construction leads away from the latter, accompanied by pyramid poplars (pyramid oaks since 1864). The required tree seedlings were generally obtained from local forests, exotic species being acquired from tree nurseries in Wörlitz or Hamburg and the like. An interwoven combination of sections of differing sentimental atmospheres developed, characterised by their respective buildings, garden staffages or type of planting. The gardens were already grown over and out of fashion by 1816,

The Gothic library and marble palais in the New Gardens on the lakeside of the Heiligen See

and thus Peter Joseph Lenné (1789–1866) redesigned them as one of his first activities in Potsdam. While retaining many individual sections, the New Gardens were improved, endowed with great views and meadow areas, a modern and more logical path route, and above all, visual connections to the neighbouring gardens (Sacrow, Pfaueninsel, Glienicke, Babelsberg, Potsdam, Pfingstberg). Despite small modifications during the imperial period and removal of buildings added during the time of Russian utilisation (1945–54), the New Gardens still retain the original basic layout intended by Lenné. An area of 13 ha occupied as border zone until 1990, has been restored accordingly.

Situated on the highest location in the north of Potsdam are the gardens of the Pfingstberg, east of the New Gardens. The project to erect a building there already existed in 1793, being pushed ahead by the purchase of land and big-style plans by Friedrich Wilhelm IV. Completion was only partial in 1863 due to his illness. Charming landscape gardens were created subsequently according to plans by Lenné. The existing buildings (belvedere, Pomona temple, country house and Villa Quandt) were integrated and above all, the numerous opportunities provided by the grounds for a view of the garden landscape of Potsdam, were made use of. There is a path leading to the New Gardens via the narrow garden section of a copse called Mirbachwäldchen. Great efforts were required in the lower section of the grounds after 1994, to regain the completely destroyed 8 ha of park area occupied since 1945 as "Little Russia".

The pyramid designed as ice cellar and garden staffage in the New Gardens

BERLIN-BRANDENBURG

STIFTUNG PREUSSISCHE SCHLÖSSER UND GÄRTEN BERLIN-BRANDENBURG

Sacrow

i Visitor centre
Tel. 03 31/96 94 200/201,
Fax 03 31/96 94 107

Size: approx. 26.3 ha

⊙ The gardens are freely
accessible daily throughout
the year from dawn to dusk

✕

🅿 Beyond the Luisenplatz
🚌

The Heilandskirche (Church of our Saviour) near the port in Sacrow with a view beyond the Havel of the farming estate next to the New Gardens and the Pfingstberg (Whitsun Hill)

Sacrow Gardens are situated to the north west of Potsdam, on the other side of a lake called Jungfernsee (Maiden Lake). They are harmoniously integrated in the grounds surrounding the lake (Königswald, Pfaueninsel, Glienicke, Neuer Garten). Baroque gardens were also established under Count J. L. von der Hordt, who built a Schlösschen (little palace) from 1773 onwards. The gardens featured a straight avenue of chestnuts leading from a circular flowerbed with sundial near the palace to a massive summerhouse on the Havel. Next to this, were two mulberry plantations and a carp pond. Count August Ferdinand von Haeseler, a stepson of Hordt, came to be owner of Sacrow in 1787, commencing with the establishment of a landscape garden in 1800. A former inn was used as hermitage with ice cellar, a large greenhouse was added to the palace, and the mulberry plantations gave way to kitchen gardens. Completely new however, were the numerous curvy walking paths on either side of the old avenue. After a series of owners disinterested in the park, Friedrich Wilhelm IV bought Sacrow immediately after his succession

to power in 1840, in appreciation of its excellent location. Construction of a church known as the Heilandskirche (Church of our Saviour) began immediately afterwards on the tip of land jutting furthest into the Jungfernsee, according to plans by Ludwig Persius. Lenné produced plans for the beautification of the gardens, which were however only implemented in the most important places, for financial reasons. The paths generally remained as they were, and only limited accentuating planting was carried out. The groups of deciduous trees and shrubs smartening up the road to Krampnitz were also visible from the grounds located on the other side of the Havel. After an unspectacular century and years of extensive farming of the Sacrow Gardens, the turning point came with the erection of the Berlin Wall from 1962; 8 ha of park area were completely destroyed, the rest became derelict due to lack of care and various constructions built by a customs dog school. On transferral to the Heritage Trust, removal of these additions and restoration of the gardens commenced in 1994.

Babelsberg Park

Lenné completed the design of the park landscape of Potsdam with the creation of the classical landscape park Babelsberg from 1833 to 1839. Records show that Pückler was actively involved from 1842 to 1868. Kindermann jun. designed the area newly acquired in the year 1865, situated in the southwestern plain.

On his marriage to Princess Augusta, Prince Wilhelm was given permission by his father in 1833 to build a palace on the Babelsberg. He received a leasehold on 72 ha. The location selected for the palace was halfway up the north slope with a view of the lake landscape of Potsdam. Schinkel was commissioned to construct a palace in the English Neogothic style, the first part of which was completed in 1835 under Persius.

Lenné's design of the park concentrated on the creation of wide park regions, a wide-meshed network of carriageways; the areas in close vicinity of the palace featured a bowling green and the preliminary stages of a pleasure ground.

Persius made designs for the extension of the palace, which was to be completed in 1849 by Strack and Gottgetreu after his death.

The palace was related in terms of height to pleasure ground and bowling green, by the creation of an exedra in the east, the blue and golden terraces, as well as the porcelain terrace to the north of the palace (Pückler and Persius) and the Voltaire terrace to the south (Strack).

Pückler rounded off the network of carriageways, making it more intricate by the creation of narrow footpaths, redesigned park areas and view projections by Lenné, and created a host of new images by skilfully placing woody plants. He implemented new planting methods. He had planting carried out particularly densely, with the intention of removing and reusing the woody plants. There is evidence to show that trees were trimmed with the aim of obtaining large shrubs. With the construction of a machine house and water reservoir in 1845, Pückler was able to create artificial lakes such as the "Black Sea", ponds, fountains and brooks. A water network used for nurturing the woody plants, lawns and flower areas was established. A significant improvement in growth on the difficult sandy soil was thus achieved.

ℹ Visitor centre
Tel. 03 31/96 94 200/201,
Fax 03 31/96 94 107

Size: approx. 136 ha

☉ The gardens are freely accessible daily throughout the year from dawn to dusk

✳

🅿 Mühlenstraße, Altnowawes
🚌

Double page:
Bowling green in front of Palace Babelsberg with colonnades of the Glienicker bridge and the Großen Neugierde (Great Curiosity)

Flatow tower as seen from the view of the Teltow

Other buildings such as palace kitchen, small palace, royal stables, sailor's lodge, Flatow tower, coachman's lodge, Havel house, court nursery gardens, Gerichtslaube (a summer house) and porter's lodge, made up, together with the Borkenhäuschen (a cottage), the pillar of victory and the General's bench, the varied scenery of the park.

Kindermann created the Great Lake and wide park areas in the plain, extending Pückler's spatial and axial structures to the landscape beyond.

In the artistic hands of Lenné, Pückler and Kindermann, the park grew over a period of 55 years during a series of several phases of extension, from a Prince's Garden to an Imperial Park encompassing an area of over 100 ha.

After the Emperor's death, failure to recognise the artistic value of Park Babelsberg resulted in increasingly severe neglect, finally culminating in its becoming greatly overgrown after 1945. The construction of the Richterschule (judge school) and the Berlin Wall resulted in considerable damage done to an area of about 40 ha.

Restoration efforts for the preservation of historical monuments have been in progress since 1960. Former neighbouring areas have been reincorporated since 1990. The significance of the palace and garden ensemble was acknowledged with by the recognition as World Cultural Heritage. The intensive fusion of park and landscape may again be experienced today, from restored paths through areas with replenished tree and shrub structures.

Flower beds with diverse borders and planting in the pleasure ground of Palace Babelsberg

Glienicke

Park Glienicke lies in the centre of the park landscape of Berlin-Potsdam. Initial gardens were created in 1796. In 1816, the owner of the gardens, Minister President Hardenberg commissioned Joseph Lenné, who was in his first year of service in Potsdam, with the transformation of the regular orchard terraces near the palace into a pleasure ground. Lenné created a natural terrain with moulded valleys, gentle elevations and exemplary path design, presenting surprising views of the city of Potsdam and down to the depths of the Havel lakes, moreover being considered a prime example of Lennésque garden art. Under the successive owner of 1824, Prince Carl of Prussia, Lenné was able to transform the entire country estate into a park. He divided Glienicke in accordance to the classical zones of flower gardens, pleasure ground and park, and provided it with a large bypass road. Inspired by Fürst Pückler, the Prince had the pleasure ground decorated with flowerbeds bordered in a basket-like fashion, and these have been restored since 1981. Only the smaller part of the park around the palace belongs to the Heritage Trust.

i Visitor centre
Tel. 03 31/96 94 200/201,
Fax 03 31/96 94 107

Size: approx. 7.3 ha

☉ The gardens are freely accessible daily throughout the year from dawn to dusk

✗

🅿 Königstraße,
near the parking area

🚌

The Plinius bed with Diana in front of the monastery yard in Palace Gardens Glienicke

The praying youth in front of the casino in Palace Gardens Glienicke

The pleasure ground of Palace Glienicke with a view of the Jungfernsee (Maiden Lake)

Pfaueninsel (Peacock Island)

Two characteristics distinguish Peacock Island with its 67 ha, from the other gardens. For one, garden and island being identical, with only one access route by ferry, the short ride results not only in the feeling of suspension from everyday life, but also in keeping dogs and bicycles at bay. For the other, it is the wilderness and ancient stock of trees with about 400 picturesque oaks, which already existed and were purposely incorporated in the design of the gardens. These were the prime feature dictating path design and placement of shrubbery groups, not only in the original design by J. A. Eyserbeck, but also during later rearrangements by Peter Joseph Lenné and J. A. F. Fintelmann. The King of Prussia Friedrich Wilhelm II was inspired to take possession of the island as garden grounds in 1793, by descriptions of the paradise-like atmosphere of the popular South Sea Islands discovered during journeys in the second half of the 18th century. The Otahaitan Cabinet in the North Tower of Peacock Island Palace bears witness to Peacock Island having been considered equivalent to its far away sisters. On approaching from Potsdam by ship, Peacock Island is immediately recognised by the white Schlösschen (little castle) built in 1794 visible far and wide, with its characteristic towers and their connecting bridge. The location of the half-timbered construction of the little castle on the western tip of the island was especially chosen because of this view from the New Gardens and from the boat. When waiting by the landing stage today, one may only see a modest castellan house and a ferry

i Visitor centre
Tel. 03 31/96 94 200/201,
Fax 03 31/96 94 107

Size: approx. 60.2 ha

☉ The gardens are freely accessible daily throughout the year from dawn to dusk and may be reached by ferry against payment of a charge

✕

🅿 Beyond the public inn called Gasthaus Zur Fähre

🚌

The fountain on the water reservoir of the Pfaueninsel (Peacock Island)

STIFTUNG PREUSSISCHE SCHLÖSSER UND GÄRTEN BERLIN-BRANDENBURG

house reminiscent of a fishing hut on the opposite bank densely covered with trees and shrubs. Once on the island, walking past the blue hydrangeas through a steep pergola walk upwards to the top of the island, one is surprised by a flower garden enclosed by a pergola and the little castle appearing from behind. A side path leads to an idealised Swiss house built by the architect Karl Friedrich Schinkel. One's glance may drift from the little castle over the Havel's wide expanse of water to Glienicke, the New Gardens and Sacrow. Extending to the east of this is open meadowland bordered with picturesque tree outlines, from which a view extending more than 1.5 km is directed to the white ruin of the Meierei (dairy). The royal menagerie was housed in the centre of the island from 1824 to 1842, which provided the basic stock for the Zoological Gardens of Berlin. Only an aviary and a water bird pond in the centre of the island still recall these times. Opposite Prussia's earliest rose garden dating from the year 1821 and restored in 1989, stone pedestals and beds planted with historical leafy plants bear testimony to the large palm house destroyed by fire in 1881. The northern part of the island with the dairy built in Gothic style in 1795 and its wide meadows has been retained in its original form as decorative farming area.

Pfaueninsel palace – view towards Sacrow

Palace Gardens Charlottenburg

The palace of Lietzenburg was built as summer residence for Sophie Charlotte (spouse of Elector Friedrich III) by Nering from 1696–1699, in rural surroundings west of the Tiergarten (Zoological Gardens). The gardens were the first German gardens to be designed in the French style under Simon Godeau, a student of Le Nôtre.

Sophie Charlotte selected the ground floor of the palace for her private rooms. Three view axes lead from the middle Oval Hall to Palace Schönhausen and Oranienburg and the citadel Spandau. Situated below the terrace, was the sun-facing broderie parterre, divided into eight compartments lined with avenues of trees comprising four rows to the east and west, which enclosed a large water basin towards the north. The inner rows of trees were bordered with hedges towards the parterre. To the east and west of the parterre were boskets. Maille alleys and canals continued from the northern part of the western bosket. A further elongated parterre, concluded by a garden hall, was situated towards the west of the palace. Vases, sculptures and exotic plants decorated parterre and terrace.

ℹ Visitor centre
Tel. 03 31/96 94 200/201,
Fax 03 31/96 94 107

Size: approx. 56.6 ha

☉ The gardens are freely accessible daily throughout the year from dawn to dusk

✕

🅿 In front of the palace

🚌

The dark spruce avenue to the mausoleum in Palace Gardens Charlottenburg

Elector Friedrich III came to be King Friedrich I of Prussia in 1701, and the sudden death of Queen Sophie Charlotte in 1705 put an end to the social, cultural and artistic heyday of Lietzenburg. Friedrich I called the palace Charlottenburg. Extension of the palace building was continued.

Charlottenburg gained importance under Friedrich II in 1740. Linden trees were planted in the gardens and the parterre border was planted with flowers. Statues were put up and the orangery parterre to the south of the orangery was lined with potted Seville orange, lemon and orange trees. The New Wing extending towards the east completed the palace complex.

Under the rule of Friedrich Wilhelm II from 1786–1797, August Eyserbeck took first measures to modify the gardens in the landscape style. The northern parts of the gardens were landscaped. The large broderie parterre was made into one large lawn area and decorated with shrubberies. Paths threaded the boskets, canals were shaped with naturally designed banks and a fashionable *aha* experience was achieved in the west of the gardens. The belvedere on the Spree

View from Palace Charlottenburg of the broderie parterre

built by Langhans in 1788, represented the major focus of the gardens with landscape character.

Steiner continued rearrangement of the gardens from 1801. Friedrich Wilhelm III approved a mutual project undertaken by Steiner and Lenné in 1818. This endowed the gardens with their actual landscape character. Lenné remodelled the bowling green (former parterre) in 1828. From 1834–1835, the Fürstingarten (Princess Gardens) to the south of the New Wing was also beautified by Lenné.

Expansion of the city from the second half of the 19th century, deprived the palace and gardens of Charlottenburg of their charming location.

Palace and gardens suffered severe damage during the Second World War. Reconstruction of the broderie parterre was opted for in the process of rebuilding. Broderie designs follow examples provided by pattern books. The northern part of the gardens, which was greatly handicapped by the Berlin-Hamburg railway line and used for allotments and rubble heaps after 1945, was re-integrated in the park design. The parterre reconstructed in the fifties was restored in spring 2001.

One of the four crowning vases on the longitudinal axis of the parterre in front of the balustrade of the carp pond

Königs Wusterhausen

i Visitor centre
Tel. 03 31/96 94 200/201,
Fax 03 31/96 94 107

Size: approx. 2.8 ha

☉ The gardens are freely accessible daily throughout the year from dawn to dusk

✕

P To the east of the Kavalier-häuser (Cavalier Houses)

🚌

The Electoral Prince of Brandenburg (since 1688 Elector Friedrich III, and from 1701 onwards King Friedrich I) acquired Wusterhausen in 1683 with the "Feste Haus" on the northern banks of the Notte, which was converted in the late 16th century and surrounded by a moat.

Kitchen gardens to the west of the palace with summer and greenhouse were divided into small plots and built on between 1830 und 1840. To the east of the palace, Electress Sophie Charlotte had a new pleasure ground created by Siméon Godeau after the French fashion for the heir to the throne Friedrich Wilhelm (King Friedrich Wilhelm I from 1713 onwards) between 1696 and 1698. A four-sectional parterre with semi-circular conclusion was lined with avenues of linden trees to the sides, the central axis beyond being emphasised by an avenue of chestnuts all the way to the Notte canal. Two Kavalierhäuser (cavalier houses) standing aslant to each other and forming an Ehrenhof (court of honour) to the palace were built in 1703 to the north of the palace island. Filling up the palace moat with soil was started in 1829, taking until 1894 to be completed. Functional buildings were constructed in the remaining garden area towards the east after 1945, a strip of land being added in 1969. The basic structure of the palace island and the former parterre were restored in 1999/2000.

Lustgarten (Pleasure Ground) Rheinsberg

i Visitor centre
Tel. 03 31/96 94 200/201,
Fax 03 31/96 94 107

Size: approx. 18.7 ha

☉ The gardens are freely accessible daily throughout the year from dawn to dusk

✕

P Opposite the garden portal

🚌

From 1737, Georg Wenzelslaus von Knobelsdorff was active in the design of the palace and gardens of Rheinsberg for the Crown Prince and later King Friedrich II until the latter's succession to the throne in 1740. In continuation of this, Prince Heinrich of Prussia created a tri-sectional garden kingdom from 1753 to 1802, lining the two lakes Grienericksee and Rheinsberger See. The atmosphere created by the fluid transition from Rococo garden to early landscape garden, unique in Germany, distinguished the pleasance. The view glides from the geometrically divided palace island to the earth terraces on the other side of the lake, being guided by two converging sloping paths to the obelisk officially dedicated in 1791, behind which a perspective avenue unique to Brandenburg displays an impressive depth of space. The two wooden flower baskets placed between marble statues of the four elements on the palace island draw attention to themselves. The park's main axis leads from the palace side wing southwards to the garden portal so characteristic of Knobelsdorff. A sunken ellipsoid chequerboard orangery parterre is included in the main axis. Between this orangery parterre and the hedge theatre created in 1753, the broken off pyramid tomb of Prince Heinrich and its self-composed French inscription rises up at the end of a dark, thoughtfully winding alleyway. At right angles to the main avenue, a long transverse avenue leads right through a "salon" towards the earth terraces. The transitional atmosphere of this garden is expressed memorably in the hedge parterre to the north, the lawn compartments enclosed by a hedge rectangle and irregular curvy borders and the unstable-looking pear-shaped vase at its centre. The picturesquely overgrown stone grotto lies at the edge of the lake. Visiting the 230 year-old linden tree avenues extending behind the earth terraces, coupled with the memorials of commemoration and grief, gives an impression of the scope of this princely garden world.

Double page:
View from the fence of trophies across Lake Grienerick towards the palace island of Rheinsberg

View from the parterre on palace island of Rheinsberg of the perspective avenues towards the obelisks ▷

Park Sanssouci, Marlygarten with Flora

Source of illustrations:
Stiftung Preußische Schlösser und Gärten Berlin-Brandenburg
(Hagen Immel, Potsdam)

Saxony-Anhalt

KULTURSTIFTUNG
DESSAUWÖRLITZ

DESSAUWÖRLITZ
CULTURAL FOUNDATION

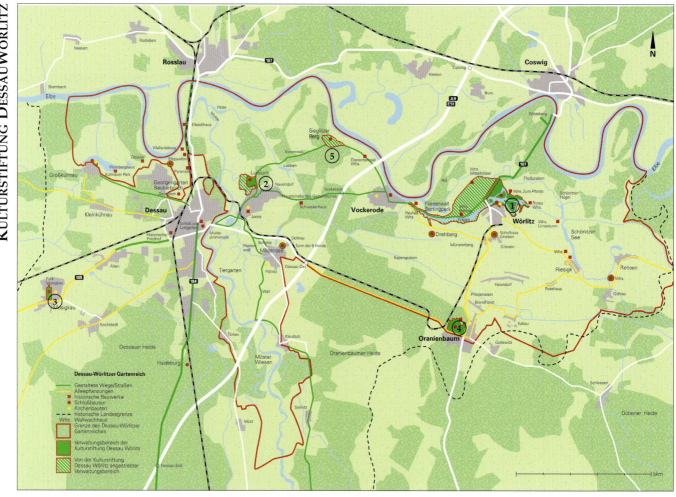

Dessau-Wörlitzer Gartenreich

- Gestaltete Wege/Straßen
- Alleepflanzungen
- historische Bauwerke
- Schloßbauten
- Kirchenbauten
- historische Landesgrenze
- Whs. Wallwachhaus
- Grenze des Dessau-Wörlitzer Gartenreiches
- Verwaltungsbereich der Kulturstiftung Dessau Wörlitz
- Von der Kulturstiftung Dessau Wörlitz angestrebter Verwaltungsbereich

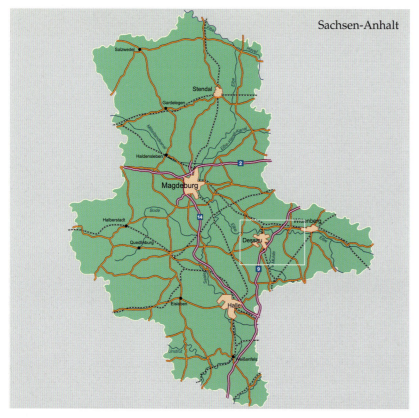

Sachsen-Anhalt

Wörlitz
   1 Gardens of Wörlitz (p. 140)

Dessau
   2 Luisium (p. 144)
   3 Baroque Gardens Mosigkau (p. 148)

Oranienbaum
   4 Baroque Gardens Oranienbaum (p. 146)

Vockerode
   5 Sieglitz Hill (p. 149)

◁ *The Faunherme near the South Gate*

Solitary oaks in the flood plain near the Kupenwall

THE GARDEN REALM OF DESSAU-WÖRLITZ

The Gartenreich (garden realm) of Dessau-Wörlitz, added to the UNESCO list of World Cultural Heritage in November 2000, is the result of extensive reform efforts initiated by the young Prince Leopold Friedrich Franz of Anhalt-Dessau (1740–1817) soon after assuming the rule of his small model state in 1758. In addition to the new orientation of the mini state with regard to all areas of life, these England-orientated ideas committed to Humanism and the Enlightenment, allowed the progressive development of a garden kingdom extending gradually over the entire area of the land. 145 square kilometres – about one quarter of the beautification of the land realised originally by the Prince, has been preserved until today and put under a preservation order.

The Prince was able to realise the aesthetic renewal of his land with the help of numerous assistants, who created a new infrastructure for the entire step-by-step gro-

wing work of art. The Prince and his advisor Friedrich Wilhelm von Erdmannsdorff (1736–1800) were inspired by Grand Tour travel impressions gathered in Europe, but mainly by repeated impressions of the landscapes and manor houses of Southern England. They attempted to transfer the effect of these creations to Anhalt-Dessau's water-rich meadowland along the Elbe and Mulde. Gardeners, foresters and farmers opened up a new terrain for the implementation of the new English art of landscape gardening in Dessau-Wörlitz, the first on the European continent: analogous to the Thames landscape around London, a combination of useable garden, forest, water, meadow and field areas was created in Anhalt-Dessau, divided by avenues, dikes, ditches and roads, appearing to be one enormous continuous garden. The landscaped parks created therein, were the highlights of a landscape design production featured like the pearls on a string, threaded along the newly established paths and roads predominantly decorated as fruit tree avenues. Wörlitz played the role of both target and highlight of all routes leading away from the Dessau residence towards the east, and was at the same time the key focus of the enlightened programme presented. Further important landmarks were the gardens of Kühnau, the Georgium and the Luisium, the Waldeinsamkeit (Forest Solitude) on the Sieglitzer Berg and the Bertingpark, about half an hours' ride away on horseback. The Baroque gardens of Oranienbaum and Mosigkau were included in the beautification of the land, and the hunting grounds around the Haideburg, the Tiergarten (Zoological Gardens) with the New Promenade and the impro-

vements carried out between the Poetenwall (Poet's Wall) and the Turm der acht Winde (Tower of Eight Winds) also numbered among the more intensively designed locations in the newly fashioned landscape.

With 209 hectares, the majority of the historical garden complex of the garden kingdom has been allocated to the DessauWörlitz Cultural Foundation, which is to be elaborated on in greater detail below. The Georgium, the gardens created for the Prince's brother Johann Georg, as well as the Tiergarten located to the east of Dessau and the landscape park Kühnau to the west, have been looked after by the city of Dessau for more than half a century.

The guardhouse Limesturm (Limes Tower) on Lake Schönitzer

Herd of animals on the paddock near the Luisium

Fruit bloom in the garden kingdom

Gardens of Wörlitz

i Kulturstiftung
(Cultural Foundation)
DessauWörlitz
Schloss Großkühnau
06846 Dessau
Tel. 03 40 / 64 61 50
Fax 03 40 / 64 61 510
www.gartenreich.com
ksdw@ksdw.de

Size of the grounds: 113 ha

⊘ Freely accessible
throughout the year
Country house Wörlitz:
Open April–October
Gothic House Wörlitz:
Open April–October

✕

P

The gardens of Wörlitz created to the east of Anhalt-Dessau represent the chronological starting point and aesthetic climax of the improvement measures carried out in the Gartenreich (garden realm). They are divided into five individual gardens, which have grown into the surrounding landscape peripheral to the palace, separated by water, in particular Lake Wörlitz, and linked to one unit by means of bridges, garden sections and interrelated views. Prince Franz, his friend and advisor Erdmannsdorff and the gardeners Neumark, Eyserbeck and Schoch (the elder) who were involved began their work in close proximity to the as yet Baroque palace and gardens in 1765, immediately after returning from their first journey to England. Their initial approach towards their design project was still immature and small-scale.

Over a period of roughly 35 years, the grounds had developed into an area of approximately 112 hectares by around 1800, seamlessly merging into the surrounding landscape without any fencing. Schoch's Garden and the Weidenheger were established between 1770 and 1790 adjoining north of the Palace Garden and Neumark's Garden, located south of Lake Wörlitz, and the New Gardens to the east in the 1790's. Almost eighty thousand visitors come to the gardens every year. They are intended to be experienced as a sequence of three-dimensional scenes presenting themselves to the visitor along a specific path as a deliberately staged programme. Something new (or a different effect) may be discovered by the

The Phallus bed near the Flora Temple is directed towards the Gothic House

visitor behind every bend, eliciting feelings of surprise and joy. The interest of the stroller is to be aroused in this manner, making him curious for more – the visitor is meant to learn.

Beauty was combined with utility, and the attractively fashioned gardens were used as fields, pasture, and meadowland and for the cultivation of fruit, similar in function to the surrounding land. The animals and human beings actually living there – the reaper in the corn, the washing woman by the lakeshore or the fisherman on Lake Wörlitz – were also part of the created scenes, playing a live role as it were. The most brilliant architectural solutions of earliest Neogothic palace construction in Germany out of the over 40 buildings and garden architectural objects, are represented by the country house (1769–1773), Erdmannsdorff's foundation building of clas-

sicistic architecture in central Europe and the Gothic House (1773; enlarged several times until 1817).

As central Europe's earliest still preserved gardens in the landscape style, Wörlitz and its architectural features acted as model for numerous garden-works-of-art. However, hardly any of the copies were able to express the comprehensive enlightened-humanistic interests in an overall work-of-art encompassing garden art, architecture and plastic arts, as accomplished by Prince Franz with his creations in Wörlitz. Making this experience available again for the visitor is the aim of the restoration work in progress in the much-visited Wörlitz since 1982.

Double page overleaf:
The mighty oak on Rose Island

Temple of Venus on the Elbdeich (Elbe Dike) of Wörlitz

Luisium

i Kulturstiftung
(Cultural Foundation)
DessauWörlitz
Schloss Großkühnau
06846 Dessau
Tel. 03 40 / 64 61 50
Fax 03 40 / 64 61 510
www.gartenreich.com
ksdw@ksdw.de

Size of the grounds: 31 ha
(including the historical
stud farm)

⊘ The gardens are freely
accessible throughout
the year
Luisium palace:
Open April–October

P

The Luisium named after **Princess Luise** Henriette Wilhelmine of Anhalt-Dessau (1750–1811; née Princess of Brandenburg-Schwedt) is situated near the eastern edge of the city of Dessau in a suburb known as Waldersee today. It was most likely created to meet her private requirements, public access being restricted to two afternoons a week during her lifetime. The garden creation with its very orderly basic layout, distinguished locally as the "German Garden", contrasted with the contemporary surrounding gardens, which had all adopted the ubiquitously dominating English style of design, was renowned as the most beautiful garden in the land. This artistic creation of nature with its great variety of species and interesting stock of trees and shrubs, mixed herds of animals, birds and amphibians, is still very popular for excursions in the outskirts of the city today.

The 14 hectares of garden are split up into the eastern utility gardens, location of the gardener Johann Friedrich Eyserbeck's (1734–1818) private and work areas from where significant improvement work was organised in the Gartenreich (garden kingdom), and the actual park arranged around the lake (former dead arm of the Mulde). An orangery found its place next to the gardener's house in 1782, and a Snake House (around 1800) characterised the kitchen and fruit gardens as Neogothic staffage. The western entrance is marked by two gatehouses, behind which a sculpture of a veiled female figure forms the endpoint of a garden axis from the

View of the palace and arched bridge from the lake

palace through an artificial Roman ruin of an arch. The dominating design elements of the park accessible from the palace by a wooden arch bridge include a Flower Garden House, a grotto building and a Pegasus fountain. The landscape adjoining to the west, features a Neogothic ducal stud farm with 16 hectares of pastureland for the horses, where the Prince bred his English horses. An old star-shaped landscape feature for hunting purposes comprising five segments to the north of the palace was used for creating view axes into the landscape. Towards the south, the central axis leads to the church of Jonitz, where the mausoleum of the princely couple has found its place.

The gardens were established on the grounds of the former Vogelherd, where Prince Franz grew up as an orphan, while his uncle Dietrich of Anhalt Dessau car-ried out the business of government for him until he became eighteen. Luise received the grounds with the pavilion-style pyramid-roofed palace of simple elegance and a belvedere as a birthday present in 1774. The Princess was significantly involved in the furbishing and design of the building completed four years later. After extensive restoration work in accordance with original design, the house as well as the gardens, are again open to visitors. Restoration of the utility gardens and the orangery to original character, are also scheduled.

The Snake House serves as holiday apartment today

KULTURSTIFTUNG DESSAUWÖRLITZ

ℹ Kulturstiftung
(Cultural Foundation)
DessauWörlitz
Schloss Großkühnau
06846 Dessau
Tel. 03 40 / 64 61 50
Fax 03 40 / 64 61 510
www.gartenreich.com
ksdw@ksdw.de

Size of the grounds:: 28 ha

🕐 Park open until dusk
throughout the year

🅿

Baroque Gardens Oranienbaum

Oranienbaum, the oldest gardens of the Gartenreich (garden kingdom) of original Dutch-Baroque design, were partially reshaped in the course of improvement measures carried out at the end of the 18th century, and adapted to the surrounding landscape. The foundation stone for city, palace complex and gardens was laid in the south eastern tip of Anhalt-Dessau near Nischwitz in 1683, at the time when Princess Henriette Katharina of Anhalt-Dessau (née Princess of Orange; 1637–1808) created her "widow's seat" here. The Dutch master builder Cornelis Ryckwaert (1662–1693) also active in Prussia produced the plans for the work-of-art finished in the early 18th century. The palace was situated opposite the market place on an island surrounded by a water-filled canal, in characteristic Dutch style of building. The kitchen gardens were located adjacent to the south and the canal gardens adjacent to the north. The large tri-sectional parterre divided horizontally featured a labyrinth garden and an island garden in the side compartments. A large forest area used for hunting completed the grounds to the west.

Although Prince Franz made use of the Dutch Baroque complex, it was not much loved by him on account of his anti-Baroque attitude towards society and creative design, and consequently neglected. As late as the 1790's, he had the two parterres to the sides re-landscaped, developing out of the former island and canal gardens the still preserved only English-Chinese gardens in the style of the Swedish-English architect and garden theorist William Chambers (1723–1796) in Europe. Restoration work on the piecemeal and water-rich grounds with pagoda, teahouse, and numerous bridges and islands, began in 1991.

The wrought-iron orange tree standing on the market place of Oranienbaum refers to the family coat of arms of Orange being at the same time heraldic motif of the city. Since the foundation of the latter, the

Schloss Oranienbaum from the parterre with Dolphin Fountain

orange tree has thus been the plant characterising the gardens, determining the appearance of the parterre during the summer months. During winter, the precious citrus plants are cultivated in the orangery built by William Chambers (1723–1796) between 1812 and 1818. With a length of 178 metres, this is the longest orangery of Germany, housing more than 550 of the valuable plants at its peak in the middle of the 19th century. The collection, which has been accumulated again since 1992, is constituted predominantly of Seville oranges (Citrus aurantium) similar to the original collection, which was not able to survive the two World Wars as well as a late frost in May 1961.

The originally luxuriously furnished palace has been used as national archives since 1945. It is intended to be opened to the public after the latter's relocation and extensive restoration work. Reinstatement of the original character of the surrounding palace-island with its gardens for living in and the court of honour is also planned.

The citrus collection in the restored orangery

Baroque Gardens Mosigkau

i Kulturstiftung
(Cultural Foundation)
DessauWörlitz
Schloss Großkühnau
06846 Dessau
Tel. 03 40 / 64 61 50
Fax 03 40 / 64 61 510
www.gartenreich.com
ksdw@ksdw.de

Size of the grounds: 16 ha

⊘ Park open until dusk
throughout the year
Mosigkau palace:
Open April–October

Annually changing
summer exhibitions
in the orangeries

P

In the former village of Mosigkau to the west of Dessau, lies a palace intended as summer residence with a park initially designed as Rococo gardens. Princess Anna Wilhelmine of Anhalt-Dessau (1715–1780), favourite daughter of the elder Dessau and aunt of Prince Franz, commissioned the building and was the first to use it. As decreed in her testament, the entire grounds including palace and estate, were used as a foundation for noble single ladies of high rank until the year 1950, being adapted for this purpose repeatedly.

Mosigkau is one of the few preserved Rococo ensembles in central Germany. The palace building was created between 1752 and 1757, presumably under the cooperation of master builder Christian Friedrich Damm, the first gardens being designed by Christoph Friedrich Broße. The tri-sectional parterre decorated with ornamental broderies and surrounded by berceaux, required intensive care, which could no longer be warranted during the period of its function as a foundation for ladies after the death of the Princess. This resulted in the grounds being redesigned under the influence of the English landscape style in a step-wise process commencing in 1784 under Johann Gottfried Schoch to be continued by Leberecht Abel later. The character of the present day gardens is still determined by the impressive 19th century trees located in the parterre between palace and orangery. The latter houses a valuable collection of precious orangery plants, some of which are as old as the

*View of the palace
from the parterre*

The Chinese Teahouse

building itself. Adjoining to this north-south axis, are a maze and an area around a Chinese House, with a fishpond and orchard still preserved behind a summer-house in an easterly direction. Reconstruction of the former "Franzobstplantage" (Franz fruit plantation) and the kitchen gardens is being planned as part of the scheduled Baroque reinstatement measures. The cemetery of the ladies' foundation is open for viewing today, situated at the northern end of the gardens, on a former utility garden area, opposite the court of honour functioning as entrance.

Forest solitude on Sieglitz Hill

"The most charming wilderness that I know", was the comment made by the travelling garden writer Prince de Ligne in 1795 on this park situated by the banks of the river Elbe in the north of the Gartenreich (garden kingdom) between Dessau and Vockerode, described as "Waldeinsamkeit am Sieglitzer Berg" (Forest solitude on Sieglitz Hill). It is still regarded as an insider tip for the interested visitor today, since it is only accessible by foot or bicycle.

The aesthetically upgraded forest gardens located on an elevation safe from the risk of flooding, of originally approximately 23 hectares of fenced in area, was established between 1777 and 1793 along the old dike path of the Kupenwall, leading the visitor past impressive meadowland with many oaks through the flood plains of the Elbaue (river meadows). The park was also accessible by a harbour on the Elbe in those days, which used to flow

ⓘ Kulturstiftung
(Cultural Foundation)
DessauWörlitz
Schloss Großkühnau
06846 Dessau
Tel. 03 40 / 64 61 50
Fax 03 40 / 64 61 510
www.gartenreich.com
ksdw@ksdw.de

Size of the grounds: 23 ha

⊘ Freely accessible
throughout the year

right past the park prior to the drop in the water table associated with the development of the river.

Focus of the park was a small classicist palace, the Solitude, built according to a design by Erdmannsdorff between 1777 and 1783, and destroyed by vandalism in 1975. The Doric columned hall consisting of four columns was orientated towards the Elbe. The three view axes running into the park from a second garden-facing palace façade, towards a Diana statue, a Wilhelm vase and a Faun statue, have been restored again today. Sculptural garden embellishments, a hermitage, a pheasantry and a gardeners' chalet accentuated this woodland traversed by aisles of light and upgraded aesthetically by additional planting. Since these also functioned as hunting grounds, former fencing was intended predominantly to keep the stags "gathered together" in the park. The gardens could be entered and driven through by three gates: the late medieval castle gate in the east, the classicist gate with gatehouses imitating antique forms in the south, and a Baroque sandstone gate with volutes on the sides in the west built around 1791.

The castle gate on Sieglitz Hill

Source of illustrations:
Archive of the DessauWörlitz Cultural Foundation

Hesse

Staatliche Schlösser
und Gärten Hessen

Administration of Public Stately
Homes and Gardens in Hesse

◁ *Welcome to the Convent Garden of the*
former Benedictine Abbey Seligenstadt

Flora rules over Palace Park Wilhelmshöhe

PRELIMINARY REMARKS

For generations, the Administration of Stately Homes and Gardens of Hessen has been looking after those unique overall works of art and ensembles of spatial art of princely provenance, thus predominantly those residential complexes which were placed into the care of the specially founded professional administrations, the Stately Homes Administrations, at the end of the German monarchy in 1918.

The central responsibilities of the Stately Homes Administrations are comprised of the study of, the protection, preservation, presentation and communication of this important and regionally significant historical heritage, which particularly include the gardens and parks of the former residences of secular and ecclesiastical princes.

It is our aim to arouse your interest and invite you to visit our 'glimpses of paradise on earth' in Hessen with the following illustrated presentation. 400 years of superb 16th to 19th century garden art are reflected by these 10 gardens: an intimate monastery garden in the former Benedictine abbey Seligenstadt, a cultivated landscape in Kassel with Baroque character, the residences of Karlsaue, Wilhelmshöhe and Wilhelmsthal as end and intersectional points of a network of avenues, or a sentimental English landscape park in the former princely spa Wilhelmsbad in Hanau, to name but a few. Appreciate and enjoy our gardens throughout the change of seasons of the year and experience the benefits derived from our professional motivation in the preservation and communication of this important cultural and natural heritage for future generations. Allow us to offer you a warm welcome as our guest.

STAATLICHE SCHLÖSSER UND GÄRTEN HESSEN

i 34379 Calden 1
Tel. 0 56 74/68 98
Fax 0 56 74/40 53
www.schloesser-hessen.de
info@schloesser.hessen.de

Size of the park: 35 ha

⊘ Daily until dusk
Waterworks:
From Ascension Day to
3 October inclusive, always
at the end of a palace tour
Special guided tours:
by prior arrangement with
the branch office of the
palace and palace park,
Aussenstelle Schloss und
Schlosspark Wilhelmshöhe
(Tel. 05 61/93 57-0;
Fax 05 61/93 57–111)

🖭

🅿 In front of the palace

DB Continue by bus

Previous double page:
View of the Corps de Logis and
kitchen wing of the palace from
the canal framed with sculptures

Grotto at the end of the canal

Palace Park Wilhelmsthal, Calden

Close to the village Calden, north west of the Wilhelmshöhe, the Governor and later Landgrave Wilhelm VIII of Hessen-Kassel (ruled 1751–1760), had a summer residence built between 1743 and 1761. The pentagonal complex consisting of a three-winged palace and generous regular park with axes extending fan-like from the palace to the east, sometimes far into the landscape, is the work of Francois de Cuvillies and Johann August Nahl. Redesign of the landscape took place under Wilhelm IX (ruled 1785–1821) – Elector Wilhelm I from 1803 onwards – by the court gardeners August Daniel Schwarzkopf, Karl and Wilhelm Hentze during the years 1796–1813. Winding paths, large areas of lawn and naturally growing groups of trees and shrubs in the gently fashioned terrain, formed a uniquely interwoven landscape. Parts of the Baroque axial system were however still retained. The central axis leads to the west from the palace via the entrance area designed in 1764 – a circular *bowling green* surrounded by trees – and further outwards, linking the summer residence with the Tiergarten (Zoological Garden) beyond the border of the park. The park's elaborate southeast axis with canal, grotto, figure ornaments and water basin, was completed by 1756. Sections of this were reconstructed near the grotto – the only building remaining after the Rococo garden was redesigned – and the canal in 1962, conveying an impression of the original magnificence today. The palace constructed from 1747–1755, with its simple yet elegant façades, luxurious and multi-faceted interior design, is one of the major examples of Rococo art in Europe.

The path from the Tiergarten via the Meimbress Avenue to the palace's Court of Honour

Curvaceous paths and casually arranged thickets in the landscape park

STAATLICHE SCHLÖSSER UND GÄRTEN HESSEN

Schlosspark 3
34131 Kassel-Wilhelmshöhe
Tel. 05 61/93 57 - 0
Fax 05 61/93 57 - 111
www.schloesser-hessen.de
info@schloesser.hessen.de

Size of the park: 240 ha

Open all day
Waterworks: Wednesdays,
Sundays and public
holidays from Ascension
Day to 3 Oct. Guided tours
of the waterworks on Wed-
nesdays and Sundays at
2.00 pm, Meeting point is
the Kasse (box office) Okto-
gon. Illuminated water-
works near Hercules as well
as the aquaduct and the
Great Fountain after the
onset of dusk.
Waterworks by special re-
quests on prior arrangement
Large greenhouse: 1st Sunday in December until 1 May

⊞ – ✕ – 🅿 Palace/Herkules

DB – 🚌 Bus

Palace Park Wilhelmshöhe, Kassel

A grandiose park was created between 1701 and 1714 under Landgrave Karl (ruled 1670–1730), which was described as one of the most magnificent in Europe as early as the 18th century. Impressed by the splendid Italian Renaissance gardens, he commissioned the Italian Francesco Guerniero in 1701, with the planning and creation of gigantic grounds on the eastern slope of the Habichtswald (Hawk Forest). Completed were only the enormous octagonal palace with the crowning figure of Hercules and the upper third of the cascade. After the death of Landgrave Karl, the mountain Karlsberg named after him, remained unchanged for decades. From 1763 to 1785, under Friedrich II (ruled 1760–1785), a labyrinth-like juxtaposition of various 'natural' scenes was created, accessible by means of winding paths and fitted with numerous buildings. Court gardener August Daniel Schwarzkopf however left the overall Baroque concept untouched. The Chinese village "Mulang", the Egyptian pyramid, the Sybil grotto, the Mercury temple and the Eremitage of Socrates have been preserved from this period. The landscape was redesigned under Landgrave Wilhelm IX, Elector Wilhelm I from 1803 onwards, (ruled 1785–1821). An idealised natural landscape was gradually created around the Baroque cascade axis by making use of naturally existing conditions. The architects Heinrich Christoph Jussow, Simon Louis Du Ry and the water artist Karl Friedrich Steinhofer added the Steinhöfer waterfall, the devil's bridge, the aqueduct, charming cascading courses and the Lac. These creations were in line with the romantic feeling of a landscape garden, as well as the Löwenburg (Lion Castle) built from 1793 onwards, a medieval knight's castle in ruin style, which represents a significant documentation of the period between revolution and restoration. The name WILHELMSHÖHE refers to palace and park, ever since the three-wing palace rebuilt new starting in 1786, was crowned with a pediment bearing this inscription in 1798. In 1822, Wilhelm II (ruled 1821–1831) had the Plant House, one of the earliest iron-glass constructions of Germany, built by Johann Conrad Bromeis. The unity of the grounds in the sense of an English landscape garden still existing today is the admirable achievement of the court master gardener Wilhelm Hentze.

Double page overleaf:
Baroque residential landscape between
the Hercules palace and the city of Kassel.

One of the many cascades of Palace Park Wilhelmshöhe

Vergil's burial monument

Pluto Grotto, with Devil's Bridge in the background

State Park Karlsaue Kassel

In the 16th century, Wilhelm IV (ruled 1567–1592) had a pleasure ground created in the Fulda valley, linked to his city palace by a bridge. A garden came to exist around a summerhouse built in 1568, which was characterised by the Landgrave's passion for collecting rare and exotic plants. This was divided in a chequerboard manner, richly embellished with sculptures, fountains and hedge arches. Landgrave Moritz 'the scholar' (ruled 1592–1627), was able to take possession of further large areas of meadow land, promoting the development of his father's grounds. The "Moritzaue" (Moritz Meadow) continued to be enriched artistically and botanically until the middle of the 17th century. The pleasance was integrated in the new Baroque design of the meadow in the 18th century under Landgrave Karl (ruled 1670–1730). The old summerhouse was replaced with today's orangery palace with sala terrena in the outskirts of the meadow. Of the generous enlargement of the orangery planned towards the south, using Marly-

Le Roi as model, merely a marble bath (1722–1730) and a kitchen pavilion (1765–1770) were realised. The small 16th century pleasure ground was retained to the north of the orangery whilst Landgrave Karl had a similar, richly equipped orangery garden created to the south. Based on French models, fan-shaped grounds were created under direction of master gardener Johann Adam Wunsdorf at the beginning of the 18th century. The meadow named KARLSAUE after its creator was enclosed by water canals on the sides, which met in a cloverleaf pattern in the south. The kitchen gardens were outside the northern "kitchen ditch". The southern "Hirschgraben" (Stag Ditch) derived its name from the Tiergarten (Animal Garden) lying on either side. An avenue was created along the central axis in 1710, leading towards a large pool. Swan Island, decorated with a small cupola temple today, was created in the midst of this pool built from 1722 onwards. Towards the west this was completed by a small pool finished in 1730, the island

ℹ Auedamm 18
34121 Kassel
Tel. 05 61/1 88 09
oder 9 18 89 50
Fax 05 61/1 24 16
oder 9 18 89 53
www.schloesser-hessen.de
info@schloesser.hessen.de

Size of the park: 150 ha

⊙ Park open throughout
the day
Island Siebenbergen:
1. 04 . – 3. 10.: daily from
10.00 am – 7.00 pm
Guided tours by prior
notice and arrangement.

▦

🅿

🚋 Straßenbahn (tram), bus

◁ *Waterfall by the Devil's Bridge*

View of Siebenbergen (Seven Hill) Island from the edge of the basin

STAATLICHE SCHLÖSSER UND GÄRTEN HESSEN

Double page overleaf:
The orangery palace with adjacent
bowling green with the Marble
Bath in the background on the left

Summer bloom
on Seven Hill Island

therein was named Siebenbergen (Seven Hills) due to the nature of its terrain. After large areas of the orangery gardens were destroyed during the occupation of Kassel in the Seven Year War, they were replaced with a large lawn parterre designed as a bowling green. Under the direction of court gardener Daniel August Schwarz-kopf, first typical Baroque elements such as the hedge theatre, cascade, and grotto started to disappear from 1793, small geo-metrical basins and sections of the rigid canal border being filled in with earth. Court gardener Wilhelm Hentze imparted the Karlsaue (Karl's Meadow) with its

actual landscape character from 1822. The design of the outer frame and the Baroque axes were retained. He developed land-scape garden structures within this frame-work. Hentze's special merit was the cre-ation of "Seven Hill Island", which turned out to be a gardening jewel. The park was severely damaged during the Second World War. This damage could be re-paired to a great extent in time for the Fed-eral Garden Show in 1955, in the course of which part of the meadow slopes were turned into slopes of roses by Hermann Mattern. The orangery palace was resto-red for the Federal Garden Show in 1981.

Former circular riding course

View of the Rundtempel (Round Temple) on Swan Island from the edge of the large basin

Palace Park Bad Homburg vor der Höhe

STAATLICHE SCHLÖSSER UND GÄRTEN HESSEN

i Schloss
61348 Bad Homburg
vor der Höhe
Tel. 0 61 72 / 92 62-148
Fax 0 61 72 / 92 62-147
www.schloesser-hessen.de
info@schloesser.hessen.de

Size of the park: 13 ha

⊙ 31. 10. to 31. 3.:
from 8.00 am until dusk
1. 04. to 30. 10.:
from 8.00 am until 8.00 pm
Guided tours and seminars
are available

⊞

P

🚌 S-Bahn (tram),
U-Bahn (subway)
Bus

Mid and late medieval castle buildings and today's Schloss Homburg have been seat of the Landgraves of Hessen-Homburg since 1622, and subsequently summer residence of Prussian Kings and German Emperors from 1866–1918. The "White Tower" in the upper palace court bears witness to the former medieval grounds. From 1680, Friedrich II of Hessen-Homburg (ruled 1680–1708) erected a Baroque residence in place of the old castle. Master Builder Paul Andrich created a richly furbished "Dutch-style" Baroque parterre to the east of the royal wing, at the north side of which an orangery was built in the middle of the 18th century. The landgrave's kitchen and orchards were located below the palace on the other side of the large lake. The palace park was re-landscaped as early as 1758.

Extensive gardens reaching beyond the actual palace grounds were created from 1766 under Landgrave Friedrich V (ruled 1766–1820) and his wife Caroline. They established the 2.5 km long avenue of fir trees leading to the Großen Tannenwald (Great Fir Forest). The Landgrave presented each of his sons with gardens alongside this avenue, thereby creating an entire landscape-beautifying garden axis. Friedrich VI (ruled 1820–1829) and his wife Elisabeth, who was a descendant of the English royal house, had these extended in length by the "Elisabethen-schneise" (Elisabeth Aisle) and built the "Gothic House" as Jagdschloss (hunting lodge) in the Great Fir Forest. This "landgraviate garden landscape" is currently being reactivated as a long-term project of the Regional Park Concept Rhine-Main.

View of the parterre from the entrance to the Royal Wing, shaded by a cedar of Lebanon, with the Erlöserkirche (Church of our Redeemer) in the background

One of the marvellous parterre carpet beds in front of the Royal Wing

Rose beds flanking the palace entrance

STAATLICHE SCHLÖSSER UND GÄRTEN HESSEN

View from the lower palace gardens and beyond to the palace complex with White Tower

The urn in the Elisabethenschneise of the Schlosspark

Former Benedictine Abbey Seligenstadt

i Klosterhof 2
63500 Seligenstadt
Tel. 0 61 82/82 98 82
oder 2 26 40
Fax 0 61 82/2 87 26
www.schloesser-hessen.de
info@schloesser.hessen.de

Size of the park: 3 ha

⊙ May – Sept.
7.00 am to 8.00 pm
Oct. – April
8.00 am until dusk
Guided garden tours of the
Benedictine Abbey Seligenstadt, by arrangement

The history of the monastery in Seligenstadt begins in Carolingian times, with
Ludwig the Devout presenting Einhard,
advisor and biographer of Karl the Great,
with property as a gift. In 828, he trans-
ferred the relics of St. Peter and St. Mar-
cellinus from Steinbach in the Odenwald
to the Benedictine monastery founded by
himself on the Main. The monastery
church developed into a pilgrimage place
on account of the adoration of the relics.
The town was named Seligenstadt in
840. After the confusions of the Thirty
Year War, a fundamentally Baroque
renewal of the buildings and gardens of
the monasterial city began in 1685. The
convent gardens were given a formal
structure as decorative and kitchen gardens. Game was kept in the Tiergarten
(animal garden) behind the monastery
mill. Located near the farm was a nursery
garden with an orangery built in 1757,
and a poultry farm. In the cloister court,
opposite the prelature, was the Engels-
gärtchen (Little Angel Garden) with a
group of sculptures in the midst of Mary
plants. Monastic life ended with secularisation in 1803. Many of the buildings
were used for other purposes after that.
The buildings and gardens have been
restored since 1982. The monasterial city
surrounded by a high wall bearing
espalier fruit, has become a significant
cultural centre of the region.

Double page overleaf:
View of the monastery complex
with convent garden and basilica

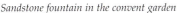
Sandstone fountain in the convent garden

HESSE

i Schlossplatz 3
35781 Weilburg/Lahn
Tel. 0 64 71/22 36
Fax 0 64 71/18 06
www.schloesser-hessen.de
info@schloesser.hessen.de

Size of the park: 3.8 ha

🕐 May – mid-October
from 7.00 am until dusk
Mid-Oct. – April
from 8.00 am until dusk
Guided tour "The Palace
Gardens" May until
September
Mondays to Thursdays
between 10.00 am and
4.00 pm by arrangement

Palace Gardens Weilburg

The palace complex Weilburg towers high above the horseshoe bend of the river Lahn, as one of the best-preserved examples of a small German residence of absolutism. At the centre is a four-wing Renaissance palace with Baroque gardens. Count Johann Ernst of Nassau-Weilburg had Weilburg developed into a Baroque residence during his reign (1675–1719). The court gardener Francois Lemaire commenced with redesigning the palace gardens in 1701. From 1702, master builder Julius Ludwig Rothweil created a complex arrangement of Baroque buildings and various garden areas around the Renaissance palace. The upper orangery with semi-circular shaped wings and a central pavilion was built in accordance with his plans, from 1703–1705. This festive garden hall linked the palace with the terrace gardens, whose parapet walls built in 1706 as protection from the Lahn valley, were crowned effectively with cast-iron balustrade sections between pedestals of marble decorated with cast-iron vases. As connection between the "upper" and "lower" terrace gardens, Rothweil built the lower orangery flanked by two flights of steps to cover this large difference in the height of the terrain. The 18th century basic structure of Weilburg Palace Gardens with dominant orangeries and terraced garden areas surrounded by supporting walls and balustrades has been preserved until the present. Design details and characteristic features of the lower terrace were restored according to the Baroque conception of garden design from 1936 onwards. Visitors may take advantage of the shade provided by a Baroque grove of linden trees and other mighty trees planted in the 19th century on the upper terrace.

*Parterre in front
of the lower orangery*

The linden tree bosket between the upper and lower pleasure ground corresponds to the original 18ᵗʰ century design

View of the upper semi-circular orangery

The promenade with Fountain Temple and Arcade Building

State Park Wilhelmsbad Hanau

i Parkpromenade 7
63454 Hanau-Wilhelmsbad
Tel. 0 61 81/8 33 76
Fax 0 61 81/8 33 76
www.schloesser-hessen.de
info@schloesser.hessen.de

Size of the park: 28.5 ha

⊘ Open all day
Guided tours by prior
notice
Special guided tours
by prior arrangement

⊞

✕

🅿

DB

🚌 Bus

The heir to the throne Wilhelm of Hessen-Kassel, who resided in Hanau from 1764–85, created WILHELMSBAD, an elegant society bath named after himself, in anticipation of financial benefit and gain in prestige for his small county. The spa grounds were created from 1777 as individual pavilions along an avenue, according to plans by the architect Franz Ludwig von Cancrin. The late Baroque ensemble of buildings was surrounded by extensive gardens, which the sovereign prince had designed in the landscape style originating from England, as one of the first German princes to do so. The interesting terrain of the former quarry provided good conditions for the development of a gently undulating English garden landscape. The spirit and intention of design of the "sensitive" early landscape grounds have been retained until today, while the once generous facilities provided for the amusement of spa and bathing guests, have virtually disappeared, apart from a large carousel and some restored playing facilities. On an island in a dammed stream called Braubach, there is a ruin-style castle with marvellous interior design: it houses the apartment of the heir to the throne and a banqueting hall in the upper storey. Lake, pyramid, hermitage, vaults, carousel and devil's bridge are further features of interest, which convey the consciously sentimental atmosphere of the romantic English landscape gardens. Wilhelmbad's lack of significance as a spa during the 19th century resulted in the cessation of further architectural developments. It is unique in Germany, as a well-preserved example of an 18th century spa and bathing resort.

Double page overleaf:
Gently moulded hills and
winding paths determine
the park's character, with
the carousel in the background

Pyramid on the island in a dammed stream called Braubusch

The heir to the throne's Eremitage in the landscape park

STAATLICHE SCHLÖSSER UND GÄRTEN HESSEN

State Park Fürstenlager Bensheim-Auerbach

i 64625 Bensheim-Auerbach
Tel. 0 62 51 / 93 46-0
oder 93 46-17
Fax 0 62 51 / 93 46 46
www.schloesser-hessen.de
info@schloesser.hessen.de

Size of the park: 42 ha

⊙ Open all day
Guided tours by prior
arrangement
Alte Wache (Old Guard-
house): Exhibition "Park
Preservation Project – State
Park Fürstenlager"
April until October
Saturdays and Sundays
10.00 am until 5.00 pm

The charming landscape park Fürsten-lager extends from an idyllic valley all the way up to the surrounding forest slopes. It all began with a spring found in the valley early in the 18th century, which was enclosed with stone some years later in 1738, thus becoming an attraction for all those in need of healing far and wide. Ludwig VIII Landgrave of Hessen-Darm-stadt (ruled 1739–1768), also convinced himself of the healing powers of the spring of Auerbach, and had a small bath-house erected in 1766. The buildings pre-served until today were created from 1787 onwards in correspondence with the con-temporary spirit characterised by the slo-gan "Back to Nature". The small village-like scenery is orientated towards the unpretentious mansion. A landscape park apparently interwoven with the border-ing forests was developed until 1807 by taking advantage of the charming topo-graphy, based on plans by the court gar-deners Carl Ludwig Geiger and Johann Heinrich Haas. Avenues run through extensive lawn areas, with numerous buildings, small architectural features, fruit plantations and vineyards, charac-terising this painting of a landscape one could walk through. The spa continued to flourish only briefly, as was the fate of many spas established out of royal good-will in the 18th century, disappearing gradually after the death of Grand Duchess Luise in 1821. The composition and special charm of this landscape park situated along the Bergstraße, a hilly wine-growing and orchard district between the foothills of the Odenwald and the lowland plain of the upper Rhine, has been retained almost entirely until today.

*View of the Fürstenlager
and the surrounding landscape*

View from the Champignon Hill: south: poplar avenues link vantage points and small architectural features in the park

Double page overleaf: View from the Temple of Friendship over the Herrenwiese (Master's Meadow) of the Herrenhaus (Master's Building)

Grotto from 1790/91 on Champignon Hill

STAATLICHE SCHLÖSSER UND GÄRTEN HESSEN

i Am Schlosspark 13–15
65203 Wiesbaden-Biebrich
Tel. 06 11 / 69 46 22
Fax 06 11 / 69 46 22
www.schloesser-hessen.de
info@schloesser.hessen.de

Size of the park: 32 ha

⊙ Open all day
Guided tours by arrange-
ment, once a month
(Wednesdays)
Exhibition "History of the
Schlosspark Biebrich" in the
orangery of the palace park
Biebrich: 1. 5. – 19. 10. 2002
Wednesdays, Saturdays
and Sundays from
10.00 am – 6.00 pm

P

DB

🚌 Bus

Double page overleaf:
View of palace with reconstructed
historical bench

Palace Park Biebrich, Wiesbaden

Palace Park Biebrich, designed by Fried-rich Ludwig von Sckell, extends to the north of the three-wing Baroque palace, and is an excellent record of English landscape gardens. The large main avenue and two small avenues extending from the east and west wings of the palace, are reminiscent of the original Baroque garden design. Construction of the horseshoe-shaped palace took al-most 40 years from 1700, under Prince Georg August of Nassau-Idstein (ruled 1665–1721) and under Prince Karl of Nas-sau-Usingen (ruled 1733–1775). Baroque gardens were created according to designs by the master builder simul-taneously responsible for the construction of the palace, Maximilian von Welsch. The Baroque gardens were redesigned as landscape gardens from 1817 under Duke Wilhelm of Nassau (ruled 1816–1839) by Friedrich Ludwig von Sckell. The tree- and bush-lined meadow valley traversing the park from north to south is regarded as the heart of the gardens. The medieval castle Mosburg was de-veloped into a romantic castle by Duke Friedrich August in 1805. Sckell had the pond created to the west of the buildings called Mosburgweiher, lining its northern curved edges with gentle hills planted with predominantly local woody vegetation. This is where the Wiesental (Meadow Valley) also ends. The natural course of the brooks called the Mosbach and the Nachtigallenbach (Nightingale Brook) enlivened the artisti-cally designed landscape. Winding paths run through the park in a particularly charming manner, alternately denying views and granting perspective axes. The park is a valuable local relaxation facility for Wiesbaden-Biebrich, due to its loca-tion in the city.

View of the small East Avenue

View of the castle Mosburg beyond the pond

View of the stock of trees and shrubs between the two main axes of the park

Prince Georg Gardens Darmstadt

STAATLICHE SCHLÖSSER UND GÄRTEN HESSEN

i Schlossgartenstr. 6b
64289 Darmstadt
Tel. 0 61 51 / 125 632
Fax 0 61 51 / 125 757
www.schloesser-hessen.de
info@schloesser.hessen.de

Size of the park: 1.8 ha

☉ 1. 03. – 31.10.:
from 7.00 am until 7.00 pm
1. 11. – 28.02.:
from 8.00 am until 5.00 pm
Guided tours by
arrangement
Special guided tours on the
1st Sunday of the month
from April until October
Arrangement by telephone
on 0 61 51 / 12 56 32,
Frau Ch. Weitzel

▤

▣

DB

 Straßenbahn (tram)

Hidden behind high walls lie the gardens named after Prince Georg Wilhelm of Hessen-Darmstadt (lived 1722–1782), used as a centre for jolly festivities far away from the ceremonial of the court of Darmstadt in the 18th and early 19th centuries. The Prince Georg Gardens were formed by merging two separate gardens into one, which can be recognised even today, on account of the principal axes meeting at right angles. In 1698, Landgrave Ernst Ludwig (lived 1678–1739) acquired a pleasure ground already established in 1624, and had a small country residence built on this land. The Prince Georg Palais was created there in 1710. The Baroque construction was flanked by a Remise (coach house) and stables, in a staggered arrangement to the south. The landgraviate grounds extended from the Palais in the north, in a fan-shaped manner southwards to the border of the gardens of Lieutenant General Johann

Rudolf von Prettlack (lived 1667–1738). The latter had a dainty summerhouse – the "Prettlack Garden House" still preserved today – built on the eastern side in 1711. In 1748, Landgrave Ludwig VIII (lived 1739–1768), was able to link his pleasance with the gardens of Johann Rudolf von Prettlack. The intimate summer residence, which was bordered by the gardens of the residential palace in the west and south, the Herrengarten (Master's Gardens), was redesigned from 1764, under Prince Georg Wilhelm. The gardens are still structured by this geometrical division today. South of the coach house and stables, the principal axis runs through a square parterre, with the four quarters arranged around a fountain, before meeting the east-west axis of the Prettlack Gardens at right angles. The Prince Georg Gardens have been restored in recent years as part of the Park Preservation Project.

View of the Tea House

Recessed seat with historical bench, view of parterre and sundial

"Utility and Beauty" – view of the main parterre of the Prince Georg Gardens

See you again in the Prince Georg Gardens of Darmstadt

Source of illustrations:
Staatliche Schlösser und Gärten Hessen (Nik Barlo Jr., Grebenstein)

Rhineland-Palatinate

BURGEN, SCHLÖSSER, ALTERTÜMER
RHEINLAND-PFALZ

CASTLES, STATELY HOMES AND
ANCIENT SITES OF
RHINELAND-PALATINATE

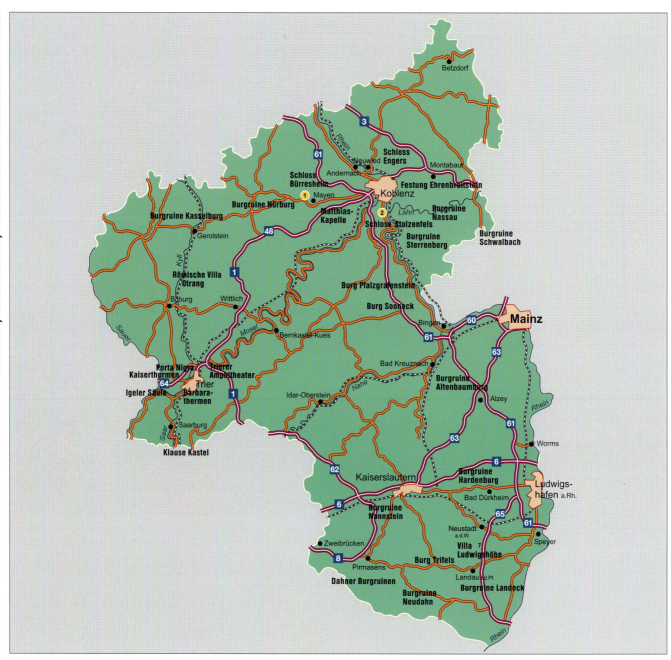

Mayen
  1 Castle Gardens Bürresheim (p. 194)

Koblenz
  2 Park and Castle Gardens Schloss Stolzenfels (p. 198)

◁ *Stolzenfels Palace, pergola gardens with the Adjutant Tower*

Stolzenfels Palace on the Rhine with a view towards Koblenz

GARDENS AND PARKS IN RHINELAND-PALATINATE

Castles, Stately Homes and Ancient sites of Rhineland-Palatinate, the organisation founded in 1998 under the umbrella of the Regional Authority for the Preservation of Historic Monuments, is responsible for the preservation and maintenance of several gardens and parks, as successor to the State Palace and Castle Administration.

These include mainly the estates of the Prussian royal house left to posterity, with Stolzenfels being an exceptional example of a romantic landscape park created by Peter Joseph Lenné. A Park Preservation Project initiated by Gustav and Rose Wörner in 1992, is being implemented there step by step. Although the environs of Castle Sooneck on the Rhine or the hermitage, Klause of Kastel located high above the Saartal, are artistically designed too, these are hardly recognisable as landscape parks at present.

The same applies for the classicistic Villa Ludwigshöhe near Edenkoben. "Palatine is my garden" was the how the Bavarian King Ludwig I explained a relinquishment of a park or garden belonging to his Villa. Design elements certainly worth exploring may also be observed there.

It was possible to reconstruct some gardens on the basis of historical designs or views, such as the Renaissance gardens of Castle Hardenburg near Bad Dürkheim and the Baroque gardens of Schloss Bürresheim in the Eifel presented here.

Schloss Bürresheim near Mayen – Castle Gardens

i Palace Administration
Bürresheim,
56727 Mayen
Tel. 0 26 51 / 7 64 40
Fax 0 26 51 / 90 24 10

⊙ 1 January until 31 March,
1 October until
30 November:
9.00 am – 5.00 pm
1 April until 30 September:
9.00 am – 6.00 pm

Final admission 45 minutes
before closing.

Closed in December.
May only be viewed
by guided tour.
The gardens are situated
outside the enclosed area.

P In front of the palace

Schloss Bürresheim looks back on 850 years of unbroken tradition as aristocratic residence. The castle was never destroyed during the numerous wars in the region to the left of the Rhine. Bürresheim was passed on in direct line without interruption as an ancestral estate between 1473 and 1938. After the lords of Breidbach took complete possession of the original Ganerbenburg from 1659, it was to become centre of a tiny direct imperial rule. The castle was imparted with a modest palatial character at the end of the Thirty Year War. Formal gardens were established on an artificially created terrace to the south of the office building, the "Amtshaus" and its representational rooms (1659–61). Its basic 17th century structure has been retained until the present. This makes the Castle Gardens of Bürresheim the oldest and to a great extent authentically preserved gardens of Rhineland-Palatinate. Only a bird's eye view of the gardens may be obtained from the castle's representational rooms. The modest access provided by a gate and steps, is intended chiefly as staff entrance.

The almost rectangular garden terrace is symmetrically divided into rectangular sections by a system of paths. The beds are box-lined; plane tree pyramids accentuate the corners. The centre of the gardens is emphasised by a four-pass fountain basin, created by the local stonemason Johann Döll of Mayen. A honeysuckle bower completes the transverse axis of the garden parterre.

The gardens are featured in relation with the castle complex on a large pictorial representation of power, a "Herrschaftsbild" as early as 1711. The illustration corresponds largely to its present state. The corners of the beds were however accentuated with roses in those days. Only one terrace survived of the utility gardens also represented on the illustration, having been redesigned as formal ornamental gardens in 1965. The symmetrical design of the terraced castle gardens is reflected only to a limited extent by the gardens of Schloss Bürresheim. The "Hortus Palatinus" of Heidelberg Castle created by Salomon de Caus after 1614, served as Germany's model.

Schloss Bürresheim, aerial photograph with castle gardens in the foreground ▷

*View of the walled castle gardens
from the Ahnensaal*

i Stolzenfels Palace
56075 Koblenz
Tel. 0261/51656
Fax 0261/5791947

☉ 1 January until 31 March,
1 October until
30 November:
9.00 am – 5.00 pm
1 April until 30 September:
9.00 am – 6.00 pm

Final admission 60 minutes
before closing.

Closed in December and on
the first working day of the
week.
Palace may only be viewed
by guided tour.

P In Stolzenfels, about
10 minutes away from the
castle by a walking path
through the permanently
accessible park.

Park and Castle Gardens of Schloss Stolzenfels

Well aware of his enthusiasm for the Rhine valley and its historical buildings, the city of Koblenz presented the Prussian Crown Prince and later King Friedrich Wilhelm IV with the ruin of the electoral Castle Stolzenfels in Trier in 1823. A wide view of the landscape including cities, castles and churches presented itself from there, high above the Rhine, opposite to its confluence with the Lahn.

The Crown Prince merely planned a romantic ruin park at first: paths were extended and made more attractive by means of additional planting. Reconstruction of the ruin began in 1836. The royal couple attended the glamorous official opening ceremony in 1842, the chapel also being completed in 1847. Karl Friedrich Schinkel was entrusted with the artistic direction, suceeded by August Stüler in 1841.

While the building and its fittings, and also the gardens in and around the castle were largely unchanged, the artistically designed landscape park fell into oblivion and became gradually overgrown. The original concept is now becoming increasingly apparent thanks to the work of the Park Preservation Project.

Park and gardens are creations of Peter Joseph Lenné. Although there are no existing plans signed by him, each of the gold-plated leaves of the laurel wreath carried in front of his coffin in 1866 bore the respective names of his creations, and 'Stolzenfels' was among them. The director of horticulture Maximilian Friedrich Weyhe of Düsseldorf and his son Wilhelm Augustin Weyhe, inspector of horticulture in Engers, were responsible for the execution of the work.

A steep and curvaceous path through a narrow gorge and over "a Roman style" viaduct erected by August Stüler, leads up to the castle. Remnants of scattered older buildings and sculptures, originating from various different places, served as a reminder of earlier times perceived as ideal. Gardens had already existed inside the castle ruin as early as 1836. The "Pergola Gardens" completed in 1842 were located on the same site: vine overgrown pergolas, sumptuous planting beds and a fountain create a southern European atmosphere there. In contrast to the intimate style of these gardens, the garden's parterre opens up before the summer hall, the central focus of which is a fountain crowned by a Prussian eagle, the latter having being created by Christian Daniel Rauch. From here a breathtaking view of the Rhine valley may be enjoyed.

Drive towards the palace with the viaduct built by August Stüler

Stolzenfels Palace, garden parterre in front of the summer hall

Garden parterre and palace church, aquarelle by Caspar Scheuren

BURGEN, SCHLÖSSER, ALTERTÜMER RHEINLAND-PFALZ

Stolzenfels Palace,
view of the pergola gardens

Source of illustrations:
Landesamt für Denkmalpflege Rheinland-Pfalz, Mainz
Heinz Straeter: p. 191, 196, 197, 198
Michael Jeiter: p. 194
CeKaDe: p. 195

Saxony

STAATLICHE SCHLÖSSER,
BURGEN UND GÄRTEN SACHSEN

PUBLIC STATELY HOMES, CASTLES
AND GARDENS OF SAXONY

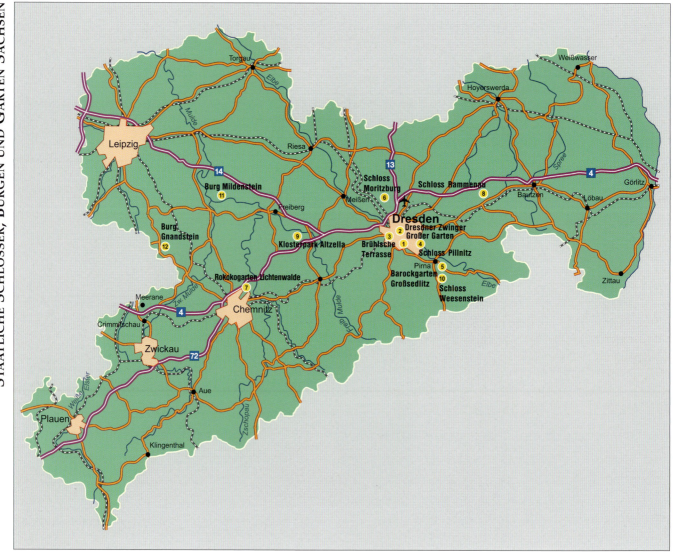

Dresden
1 Great Garden (p. 202)
2 Zwinger Gardens (p. 206)
3 Brühl Gardens (p. 208)
4 Pillnitz Palace Park (p. 211)

Heidenau
5 Großsedlitz Baroque Garden (p. 215)

Moritzburg
6 Cultural Landscape Moritzburg (p. 218)

Lichtenwalde
7 Rococo Garden (p. 220)

Rammenau
8 Palace Gardens (p. 223)

Nossen
9 Monastery Park Altzella (p. 224)

Müglitztal
10 Palace Gardens Weesenstein (p. 226)

Leisnig
11 Miruspark Mildenstein (p. 228)

Kohren-Sahlis
12 Castle Gardens Gnandstein (p. 229)

◁ *Mosaic fountain in the Great*
Garden by Hans Poelzig, 1926

Hercules in the Baroque garden of Großsedlitz

Garden art in Saxony

Gardens are essential components of old cultivated landscapes. They represent the link between the existing natural spatial environment and human creativity. Charming landscapes especially favour the creation of gardens. For this reason, Saxony not only is a country of palaces and castles, but also of gardens. Numerous garden monuments are taken care of by the Palace and Castle Administrations of Saxony – including gardens in the vicinity of castles, grand Baroque parks of imposing size, or extensive landscape parks.

In most cases, the charm of the gardens lies in the harmonious composition of representative palace building and matching artistic garden design of the complete ensemble, as visitors may find in Moritzburg, Pillnitz, in areas of the Great Garden of Dresden and in Lichtenwalde.

The romantic monastery landscape park, Klosterpark Altzella is certainly very attractive inviting visitors to stay and enjoy, and offering an amazing botanical variety, especially in spring and autumn.

Although a palace in the original sense no longer exists in the Großsedlitz Baroque Garden, the gardens captivate by virtue of their refined design, their excellently preserved condition and their clear character, not having been overhauled by any subsequent styles. Two orangeries are an indication of their former significance as well as the still existing considerable stock of potted plants.

Lovers of relatively small grounds may also discover real gardening gems in the charming Palace Park Weesenstein located in the Müglitztal, the landscape gardens of Schloss Rammenau established around 1800, the abundance of species in the Castle Gardens of Gnandstein, or the "Miruspark" by Castle Mildenstein.

The tasks of Palace and Castle Administrations include fundamental garden-historical work, supervision of garden design in the course of constructional measures, and above all, preservation of the historical gardens in public view. Approximately 70 employees, including numerous seasonally employed staff members dedicate themselves to making our garden monuments a memorable sight worth seeing and experiencing for our visitors year upon year.

Some of the gardens presented here have been restored recently and many of them have been upgraded to an excellent condition, giving the visitor a chance to comprehend the creative intentions of both those who established the gardens and their sovereign, aristocratic or occasionally bourgeois initiators.

The Saxon Palace, Garden and Castle Administration wishes you an inspiring and refreshing stay in these "jewels" of garden art.

The Great Garden in Dresden

i Geschäftsstelle:
Großer Garten
Kavaliershaus G,
Hauptallee 5
01219 Dresden
Tel. 03 51/4 45 66 00
Fax 03 51/4 45 67 22
www.schloesser-dresden.de
info@grosser-garten-
dresden.de

Size of the grounds: 149 ha

⊙ Freely accessible
throughout the year

The Great Garden in Dresden were once among the most splendid Baroque gardens of Europe, being far larger than their namesake in Hannover. They extend over an area of almost 150 ha.

Design of the "great new garden" commenced in 1676 under Electoral Prince Johann Georg, later Elector Johann Georg III. Purchase of the required areas of land took place in several stages from 1676 to 1678 and 1687. The gardener Martin Göttler is credited with the initial plans for the gardens. Chief regional master builder Johann Georg Starke created the palais located in the centre of the garden. The building was first mentioned in 1676, the ground floor being already completed by 1679/80.

The decision of Elector Johann Georg III in November 1683, to have the garden designed "a la mode", resulted in refrainment from the originally intended Renais-

Central area of the Great Garden

sance style of design. The sections of the grounds, which were completed at that stage were transformed into Baroque gardens by Johann Friedrich Karcher. Work progressed only very slowly even after accession to power by August the Strong, which may be deduced from illustrations and designs recorded in the year 1709.

French influence is clearly evident in the arrangement of the eight pavilions in 1694, the shape given to the palais basin in 1715 and the design of the moat parterre. A creative association with Marly-le-Roi in France becomes apparent. 1720 may be considered to be the year of completion of the Great Gardens' Baroque phase of design. After destruction in 1745, 1758, 1760 and 1813, first romantic modifications were carried out after 1813 under the district administrative official von Carlowitz.

Friedrich Bouché re-landscaped the Great Garden from 1873 to 1914 with retention of Baroque basic structures. The garden were declared as "public park" after 1945 and fitted with appropriate functional areas.

In some respects, the Great Garden of Dresden share the fate of other liberal landscape parks of unrestricted use, such as the English Garden in Munich or the Tiergarten in Berlin. Due to the apparent removal of the border between art and nature, which goes hand in hand with the art of landscape gardening, many of the former artistic qualities – including those of the Great Garden - are only recognisable in part by today's visitor. The older parts of the Garden in Dresden were however not rigorously removed like elsewhere, to make room for new ideas. The existing areas kept in reserve provided enough space for the integral association of new sections.

The character of the Great Garden in Dresden has been formed in the course of four centuries. Traces of the most significant European epochs of style and design may be detected in the gardens, being interwoven to a certain extent.

Park internal railway
Please check for times, by calling
Tel. 03 51/4 45 67 95

✕

🅿

DB

🚌 Tram, bus

♿ Disabled accessibility

Decorative square with group of sculptures "Abduction of Beauty by Time" by Pietro Balestra

Neuteich (New Pond) and Drachenwiese (Dragon Meadow)

Carolasee (Carola Lake) ▷

Pavillionwiese (Pavilion meadow)

STAATLICHE SCHLÖSSER, BURGEN UND GÄRTEN SACHSEN

i Geschäftsstelle:
Brühlsche Terrasse/
Zwinger/Stallhof

Zwinger, Theaterplatz
01067 Dresden
Tel. 03 51/4 91 46 01
Fax 03 51/4 91 46 25
www.schloesser-dresden.de
info-zwinger@
schloesser-dresden.de

Size of the grounds: 5.4 ha

⊙ Courtyard:
6.00 am – 11.00 pm

✕

P

DB

🚌 Bus, Steamer, Tram

♿ Disabled accessibility

The Zwinger Gardens

The gardens located between the outer and inner city fortifications (the Zwinger, or enclosure) to the west of the Palace of Dresden, are illustrated on a city map from the year 1706.

It may be assumed that the two gardens "located near the riding house" were at the disposal of the Queen and Electoress at that time. The smaller of the two gardens shown on the city map is designated as the "Zwingergarten". It was situated to the west of the riding house immediately next to a fortification wall between the "Grosse Mönch" (Great Monk) and the "Scharfe Ecke" (Sharp Corner).

The gardens near the palace were obviously not satisfactory for the King, whose travels had made him very knowledgable with respect to garden art. Lacking in particular was the frame for setting up an orangery in keeping with the period, as found in Bose's gardens as well as in the merchant Apel's gardens in Leipzig.

A basic outline drawn by August the Strong around 1709, shows just such terracing for the "Zwingergarten". Construction of the terraces commenced in 1710, however not on the site originally intended by the King, but further to the south, directly on the incline of the fortification wall of the "Sharp Corner" towards the city. It was presumably the spatial restriction posed by the piece of permanent architecture built of wood in the Zwinger in 1709, which resulted in moving the orangery terraces to the fortification wall.

The "Royal Orangery Buildings of the Zwinger Gardens" were built in several stages from 1711–1728, in accordance with plans by Matthäus Daniel Pöppelmann. They are actually described as the "Zwinger", being world-famous as the "Dresdner Zwinger". The parterre shown in Pöppelmann's copperplate engraving of 1729, was however never realised. The area was both festival

Inner courtyard with Wallpavillion (fortification pavilion)

ground and orangery parterre until 1728. Completion of construction was accompanied by a change of interest in the King's intented utilisation. From 1728, a new orangery building was available in the Duchess Gardens as winter quarter for the orangery. However, they continued to be marvellous "summer guests" in the Zwinger Gardens. It as most likely not the lack of financial resources, but the King's keen interest in a wonderful stock of oranges, which prevented the realisation of Pöppelmann's parterre design. An arrangement plan from the year 1774 shows as many as 252 potted oranges. The area was re-worked by court gardener Carl Adolph Terscheck around 1820. Further modifications ensued in connection with the erection of a memorial for the Saxon King Friedrich August I. in 1843 and the construction of a picture gallery according to plans by Gottfried Semper from 1847–1854.

In the second half of the 19th century, court garden director Gustav Friedrich Krause added further garden elements, without taking the spatial effect of the Baroque architecture into consideration.

In 1929, Hubert Ermisch created a parterre complex in the Zwinger, modelled on Pöppelmann's plans.

Zwinger grounds in the cultural centre of the city

Decorative planting bed in front of the Semper gallery

The Brühl Gardens

i Geschäftsstelle:
Brühlsche Terrasse/
Zwinger/Stallhof

Zwinger, Theaterplatz
01067 Dresden
Tel. 03 51/4 91 46 01
Fax 03 51/4 91 46 25
www.schloesser-dresden.de
info-zwinger@
schloesser-dresden.de

Size of the grounds: 5 ha

⊘ Freely accessible
throughout the year

✕ – 🅿 – DB

🚌 Bus, Steamer, Tram

♿ Disabled accessibility

Around 1730, merely one garden existed in the bastion, Jungfernbastei of Georg Maximilian von Fürstenhof within the fortifications of Dresden, which were designed for purposes of defence. The fortifications of the city of Dresden were already in need of repair in the early 18th century. Artistic layout of the gardens took place after Count Heinrich von Brühl took possession, the latter being director general of the art collections from 1733, foreign minister from 1738 and August III's prime minister from 1746. The gardens were basically divided into three sections linked in accordance with their function and design. The western area, as a sort of "front garden" was situated in front of the Palais of Brühl. The very narrow and hedge-lined middle section provided a contrast to the spatial arrangement of the Venus-bastion.

The gardener's house was located on the bastion, alongside of which an orangery had been built with a menagerie nearby. The belvedere – built on the bastion Venusbastei – represented this section's highlight in terms of design.

The sections of the garden each have a very different three-dimensional effect, giving rise to an obvious and interesting spatial sequence between individual garden elements, the design of which is attributed to Knöffel.

Brühl, who carried out some of the King's representational duties, thus had garden areas at his disposal, providing diverse facilities for social contact and functions. The garden's 18th century architectural spatial arrangement is still recognisable today, although only rudimentarily, as a result of remodelling work of the 19th and 20th centuries, and in consequence of the effects of war (1759 and 1945).

⊖ Casemates:
April–October
daily 10 am – 5 pm
November–March
daily 10 am – 4 pm
1 January 1 – 4 pm
24, 31 December closed

Ascending stairs from the Schlossplatz (Palace Square) with the "Tageszeiten" (times of day) by Johannes Schilling

Pillnitz Palace Park

In 1694, the rule or "Standesherrschaft" of Pillnitz, together with the associated Renaissance palace and a garden known for its treasure of plants, came into the possession of the House of Wettin.

Design of the gardens lay in the hands of Anna Constantia Countess von Cosel between 1706 and 1715, after having received Pillnitz as a gift from August the Strong. She created the predecessors of today's hedge gardens, known as Charmilles. Palace and gardens reverted to the Saxon Elector and Polish King in 1718. He initiated a fundamentally new design and extension of the gardens from 1720 to 1730. The Baroque basic structure created at that time, characterises the garden's image until today. The hedge gardens and the Great Palace Gardens have been almost completely preserved in their basic form. Pleasance and playground (a coniferous garden today) have not lost their axiality, although distinct alterations were carried out in the years that followed. During the Baroque age, Pillnitz was an amusement park unique in its kind, a royal playground.

The decision of the Wettin family to use Pillnitz as a permanent summer residence involved enlargements of the palace park after 1768. The English Garden was created after 1778, fully in accordance with the taste of the Elector Friedrich August III. The Dutch Garden, which was referred to as "Botanical School" from 1800 to 1867, was established after 1785 and the Chinese Garden after 1790. Court gardener Christian Friedrich John was responsible for the care of the palace park and the botanical collections therein, from 1798 to 1832. After his death, the "botanical" gardener Johann Gottfried Terscheck was in charge of the palace park until 1865.

Today's lilac court, the Fliederhof, was established in 1828, with the first lilac planting probably commencing in 1860. The ferry section created after 1864 was to be the final extension of the palace park. Peter Joseph Lenné and Gustav Meyer were the designers of this area. The plea-

i Geschäftsstelle:
Schloss und Park Pillnitz
Schloss Pillnitz
01326 Dresden
Tel. 03 51/2 61 32 60
Fax 03 51/2 61 32 80
www.schloesser-dresden.de
info-pillnitz@
schloesser-dresden.de

Size of the grounds: 28 ha

⊙ Information centre Alte Wache (Old Guardhouse):
May – October
9.00 am – 6.00 pm
November – April
10.00 am –4.00 pm
25, 26 December
11.00 am –3.00 pm
24, 31 December closed

⊙ Park open from 5.00 am until dusk
Guided tours: Easter,
April: Sat, Sun,
May – October
Daily 11.00 am,
12.00 midday, 1.00 pm,
2.00 pm
and by prior arrangement

◁ *View of the cathedral from the Brühl Gardens*

Pillnitz, English Garden

⊙ Camellia House
during camellia flowering
Mid-February – mid-April
depending on blossoming
period
Daily 10.00 am – 5.00 pm

✕

🅿

DB

🚌 Bus, Steamer

♿ Disabled accessibility

sure garden was reworked several times in the 19th century, its present form including trees and shrubberies originating from the year 1867. The new construction of the Palm House was started as early as 1859. The "Botanical School" was transformed into a symmetrical flower garden in the years 1867/68. The planned enlargement of the stock of orangery plants necessitated the conversion of the "Ringrenn" building to an orangery in 1874. The playground was transformed into a garden of coniferous plants from 1874 until 1880.

The utilisation requirements of the Wettins in Pillnitz changed increasingly after 1768. The significance of botany gained in importance under Elector Friedrich August III, who later became the Saxon King Friedrich August I. The Baroque gardens created for amusement, came to be a royal summer residence with precious botanical collections. Both camellia and the garden of coniferous plants (also known as Koniferenhain or conifer grove), created under King Albert, are of special significance from a dendrological aspect. Court gardens director Gustav Friedrich Krause was designer of the areas created in the second half of the 19th century.

Previous double page:
Pleasure garden with Bergpalais
(Mountain Palais)

Fliederhof (Lilac Court)

Großsedlitz Baroque Garden

Großsedlitz lies on a range of hills 15 km south east of Dresden.

The Imperial Count August Christoph von Wackerbarth bought Sedlitz manor estate including the villages Groß- and Kleinsedlitz on 21st July 1719.

His intentions were to take advantage of the natural terrain by creating two gardens, which were to be linked by an avenue of lime trees. The grounds planned at the Erlichtberg offered a wonderful view of the valley of the Elbe, while, by making use of the relief of the land, the grounds of Großsedlitz provided a view of the charming landscape all the way to what is referred to as Saxon Switzerland. The endpoint of the avenue of lime trees connecting the two gardens was by a three-winged palace complex, with the side wings positioned at an obtuse angle. The central axis to the front of the palace is simultaneously the axis of symmetry, being continued southwards by an arrangement of steps. Wackerbarth planned, following the French model of garden art, to perfect the Baroque garden with individual design elements such as parterres, avenues of trees and trellises, forests and boskets, to the east and west of this axis of symmetry.

Schloss Friedrichsburg built in 1719/20 was pulled down in 1871. The little palace, Friedrichschlösschen still existing today, was built on the site of the former east wing.

Construction and completion of the upper orangery was carried out in 1720/21, according to plans designed by Johann Christoph Knöffel.

The garden came into the possession of the Elector Friedrich August I on 30th January 1723. The purchase, which was kept secret until 1726, lead to a temporary interruption of planning procedures during 1723.

First drafts for a new design of the palace and garden grounds, were presumably made by August the Strong himself, and are likely to have been influenced by his impressions gathered during the "Grand

ℹ Barockgarten Großsedlitz
(Baroque Gardens Großsedlitz)
Parkstraße 85
01809 Heidenau
Tel. 0 35 29/5 63 90
Fax 0 35 29/56 39 99
www.barockgarten-grosssedlitz.de
barockgarten@compuserve.de

Size of the grounds: 5 ha

🕐 Summer
Daily 10.00 am – 6.00 pm
Winter
Sun–Fri 10.00 am – 4.00 pm
Sat 12.00 midday – 4.00 pm
24 December closed

🍴

🅿

DB

🚋 Tram (about 20 min by foot), Bus

♿ Disabled accessibility

View from the "Naturtheater" so-called nature theatre

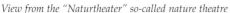

Tour". This involved both August the Strong's idea of creating a ring of palaces in the vicinity of Dresden, which were allocated to various functions of the court's festive programme, and his preference of a central building. Großsedlitz was thus intended and utilised for the annual festival of the Polish White Eagle Order.

August the Strong instructed the general manager and artistic director August Christoph von Wackerbarth with the direction of garden planning as early as 1723. In 1727, the latter entrusted Matthäus Daniel Pöppelmann, Zacharias Longuelune and Johann Chistoph Knöffel, "in order for them to develop their plans independently from one another, so that the best could then be selected from one or the other", as the King wrote in a letter.

Longuelune's great central building pro-ject, which was to be constructed behind the upper orangery, was never carried out. However between 1723 and 1727, a partial reshaping of the gardens, which until then had been completed under the direction of Wackerbarth, was carried out, designed to emphasise the avenue towards the projected central building behind the upper orangery as central axis of symmetry.

This former side axis was now redesigned as the garden's main axis of symmetry, with a planned but never completed large water cascade. The terrain of the garden, severed by a little side valley, forming 'slope and anti-slope' as it were, reminiscent of Italian Villa gardens, served as inspiration for the garden featuring the elements of a Baroque garden, even though it remained unfinished.

View from the upper orangery of the "Great Cascade" ▷

View from the quiet music, "Stille Musik"

Cultural Landscape of Moritzburg

STAATLICHE SCHLÖSSER, BURGEN UND GÄRTEN SACHSEN

i Schloss Moritzburg
01468 Moritzburg
Tel. 03 52 07/87 30
Fax 03 52 07/8 73 11
www.schloss-moritzburg.de
schloss.moritzburg@
lff.smf.sachsen.de

Grounds near the
Jagdschloss
(Hunting Castle): 8 ha
Grounds near the Fasanen-
schlösschen (Little Pheasant
Castle): 10 ha

⊙ Palace opening hours:
April – October
Daily 10.00 am – 5.30 pm
November – March
Tue – Sun
Tours:
10.00 & 11.00 am;
1.00, 2.00, 3.00, 4.00 pm
(Open Sat & Sun only in
Jan. & Feb.)
Closed 24 & 31 Dec.

✕

P

DB

🚌 Bus

♿ Disabled accessibility

The hunting seat, Jagdschloss Moritzburg was built as early as 1542 by Duke Moritz of Saxony near a place called Eisenberg (today's Moritzburg), on a rocky tip of land on the Mosebruch.

Several conversions and extensions resulted in the present-day design, reminiscent of the Loire castle Chambord. The castle built in old hunting grounds of the court near Dresden, was starting point for significant changes made in the natural terrain.

Extension of the forest Friedewald for hunting purposes was already planned and partially executed in the 16th and 17th centuries.

The cultivated landscape designated as "general work of art" however only came into existence by realisation of the complex creative ideas of August the Strong in the 18th century.

The ingenious utilisation of space provided by nature, particularly by reshaping of the pond landscape, allowed the achievement of a symbiosis between art and nature, the effect of which has survived to the present. Starting from the east-west alignment of the ensemble originating from the 17th century, a corresponding axial integration into the landscape was initially intended.

The south-north axis gained increasing importance after 1723, with the castle's main access drive being orientated towards Dresden.

The creation of a pleasure garden was started after 1726, probably according to plans by Matthäus Daniel Pöppelmann, on the northern banks of a pond connected to the island by a causeway. Progress of work was obviously slow, since the grounds were only completed in part by 1740.

Sources and findings originating from the first half of the 20th century, and particularly the shaped spruces planted along the main axis, allow the presumption that at least the inner area of the pleasure garden was created according to a design by George Gottlob Meister.

The design of the pheasant gardens created after 1769 under Elector Friedrich August III, great-grandson of August the Strong, may be considered as the highlight of the cultivated landscape of Moritzburg in terms of the programme of garden art. Since 1728, the pheasant garden lodge formed the eastern endpoint of

Schloss Moritzburg in the morning fog

the former main axis extending beyond Schloss Moritzburg. The Chinese-style little pheasant castle "Fasanenschlösschen" erected on the same site in the year 1770, became the focal centre of a "travelling scenario", which was certainly comparable to Wörlitz with regard to spatial concentration and thematic intensity. The pheasant and aviary grounds in the immediate vicinity of the little Rococo palace are still preserved in part. The Saxon "Journey by boat to Asia" is related in particular by the point of departure – harbour with mole and light tower – and the point of arrival – the Chinese Schlösschen with the Venus fountain before it. Apart from the windmill once located on the opposite bank of the large pond, the other elements featured in the "travel route" may be viewed. The so-called "maritime" area includes the Tiergarten wall with gondola houses, the fortified island securing the harbour entrance, a second also fortified island on which there was a small reed thatched cottage, the Dardanelle wall and the canal.

Fasanenschlösschen
(Little Pheasant Castle)
with canal and Venus fountain

View of the gardens from the palace terrace

Lichtenwalde Rococo Garden

**Palace and Park
Lichtenwalde**
Schlossallee 1
09577 Lichtenwalde
Tel. 03 72 06/8 13 80
Fax 03 72 06/7 38 97
www.schloss-lichtenwalde.de
info@schloss-lichtenwalde.de

Size of the grounds: 10 ha

Palace and Park:
Mid-April – October
Daily 9.00 am – 6.00 pm
November to mid-April
Daily 10.00 – 5.00 pm
The park may also be visited
after 5.00 or 6.00 pm
(entrance fee)
Palace:
Box office closes/final
admission 30 min before
closing,
Closed 24 December

Bus

Disabled accessibility

The Seven Arts

The Elector Johann Georg IV exchanged the properties in Lichtenwalde belonging to the Electoral Saxon court since 1591 for Pillnitz in the year 1694. The estate came to be property of the Imperial Count Christoph Heinrich von Watzdorf in 1722. He had the old castle complex pulled down almost completely and a new palace built. Recognition of garden design in direct relation to the new palace, corresponding to the classical principles of Baroque design is only possible rudimentarily. Establishment of the garden preserved in basic outline until today, was carried out under C. H. von Watzdorf's son, Friedrich Carl von Watzdorf, during the years 1730 to 1737. The garden, completed by 1767, are among the most famous Rococo creations of Saxon garden art. The terrain sloping downwards towards the south, is divided into terraces by three avenues/longitudinal axes. The "Great Avenue" forms the backbone of the grounds. Garden areas and attractions corresponding to the more intimate character of Rococo, are arranged to the south of this avenue, and accessible by means of longitudinal, transverse and diagonal connections. The garden became very famous chiefly on account of the waterworks and the ingenious integration of the surrounding landscape. Until today, the water required for the waterworks is pumped from a valley called the Zschopautal 90 m lower in altitude, to a reservoir located at the highest point, and distributed to 60 fountains and water basins from there. The water was originally gathered in a half moon-shaped basin below the "Sieben Künste" (Seven Arts), prior to descending to the depths as a fantastic waterfall. Around 1800, the gardens were extended under Count Friedrich II. August Vitzthum von Eckstädt by a landscape section, known as the "New Section", accompanied by simultaneous modifications of older parts of the garden. The many flat bowls lying on the lawn, equipped with simple spurting jets, referred to as "frogs",

originate from this phase of design. Unfortunately, very few of the former sculptures so characteristic of the Rococo grounds have remained intact. In contrast to the other gardens in and around Dresden, Lichtenwalde garden were only opened to strangers and visitors twice a year in the early 19th century. This was changed towards the end of the 19th century. Entrance to the garden has been virtually unrestricted for the public since then. The Konzertplatz (Concert Square) appropriate for meeting the needs and interests of those days still enjoys great popularity today. The palace fire on 1st May 1905, and the subsequent construction of the new building, resulted in modifications of the affected garden in the immediate vicinity of the palace.

The garden of today are distinctly characterised by the reconstruction work carried out in the second half of the 20th century. Its stock of trees and shrubs so vital for characterising garden structure was almost completely replaced during that time. Joint owners of the garden are the Free State of Saxony and the rural commune Niederwiesa.

View of Juno beyond the vase segment

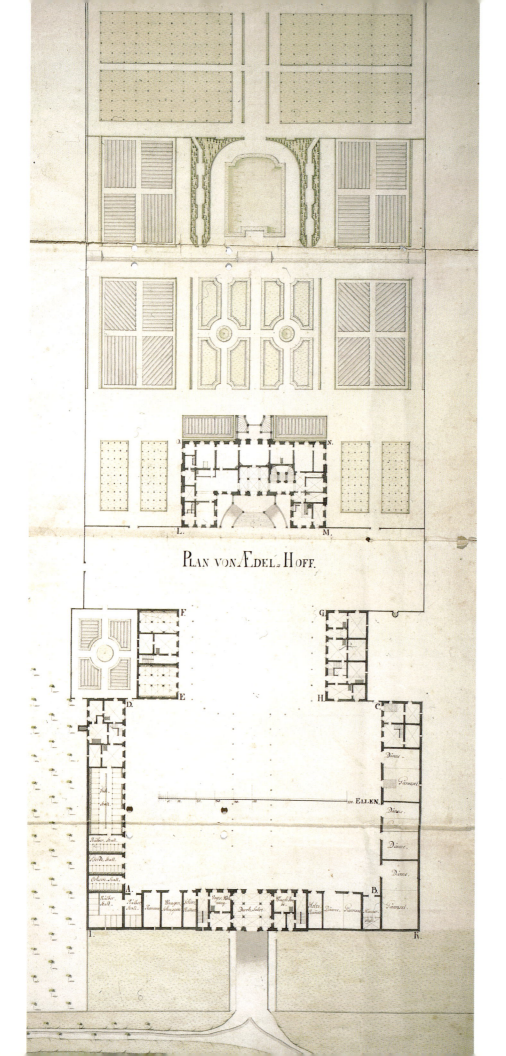

PLAN VON ÆDEL-HOFF.

*Historical design dating
from the 18th century*

Palace Gardens Rammenau

The palace grounds of Rammenau, including the associated gardens, were created by the councillor of appeal and chamberlain Ernst Ferdinand von Knoch during the first half of the 18th century. The disposition of the basic layout of the "Aedel Hof", with its farm, the so-called Meierhof before it, is very reminiscent of Baroque estates in Schleswig-Holstein. This creative connection not considered in greater detail so far, seems to be confirmed in particular by the two-storey gatehouse above the narrow entrance drive with its tower visible far and wide. Very few traces have remained of the former Baroque gardens located behind the palace surrounded by a wall 3¾ cubits high. These gardens were probably completed after Franz Joseph von Hoffmann took possession of the property in the year 1744, possibly even after his death in 1749, by his nephew Albericus von Hoffmann. The latter called himself 'von Hoffmannsegg' after elevation by the Emperor to the rank of Imperial Count in 1778. Reshaping of the garden landscape was carried out around 1800 under Johann Centurius von Hoffmannsegg or his brother-in-law Friedrich von Kleist. The natural scientist and co-founder of the Zoological Museum in Berlin, J. C. von Hoffmannsegg, owned extensive collections of plants in Dresden and Rammenau. He achieved great respect and acknowledgement in learned circles with his natural science research journeys and with the unfortunately unfinished work of his lifetime "Flore portugaise". The original harmony of the landscape gardens of Rammenau will be perceived immediately by the eye of the knowledgeable visitor. The surrounding agriculturally used land was cleverly integrated into the design. An excellently drawn, but unfortunately unsigned plan, clearly shows the intended design. It is uncertain whether the gardener Ferdinand Ludwig Vollrath trained under the Imperial Count von Pückler, was involved in planning the design. The classical character imparted to the Baroque palace in the course of re-landscaping of the gardens is remarkable.

i Barockschloss Rammenau
(Baroque Palace
Rammenau)
Am Schloss 4
01877 Rammenau
Tel. 0 35 94/70 35 59
Fax 0 35 94/70 59 83
www.barockschloss-
rammenau.com
info@barockschloss-
rammenau.com

Size of the grounds: 5 ha

☉ Summer
Daily 10.00 am – 6.00 pm
Winter
Sun–Fri 10.00 am – 4.00 pm
Sat 12.00 midday – 4.00 pm
24 December closed

✳

🅿

🚌 Bus

♿ Disabled accessibility

Landscape gardens – view of the palace

i Klosterpark Altzella
(Monastery Park Altzella)
Am Schloss 3
01683 Nossen
Tel. 03 52 42/5 04 30
Fax 03 52 42/5 04 33
www.kloster-altzella.de
info@schloss-nossen.de

Size of the grounds: 17.5 ha

⊙ March
Sat/Sun/Public holidays
11.00 am – 5.00 pm
April–October
Mon–Fri 10.00 am – 5.00 pm
Sat/Sun/Public holidays
10.00 am – 6.00 pm
November
Sat/Sun/Public holidays
11.00 am – 4.00 pm

✕

P

DB

🚌 Bus

♿ Disabled accessibility

Monastery Park Altzella

In the year 1676, 126 years after dissolution of the Cistercian monastery Altzella, work began to uncover the burial grounds of the Wettiner beneath the rubble of the former monastery church, followed by the construction of a mausoleum. Construction work under direction of chief regional master builder Wolf Kaspar Klengel, was delayed and could not be continued for a while. Work was continued after 109 years – in 1785 – under chief regional master builder Christoph Adolph Franke. The exceptionally long period of construction is not evident in the burial chapel completed in 1804, because the early classical self-contained building, received its final finish during the last phase of construction. In accordance with the trends of that time and the ideals of landscape garden art, it was originally intended to plant a grove of pyramid poplars and lime trees around the burial site. This suggested design, reminiscent of the Rousseau grave in Ermenonville was discarded. Instead, the garden artist Johann Gottfried Hübler, son of the court gardener Johann Gottfried Hübler, was commissioned in 1798, to plan appropriate natural grounds surrounding the building. After approval of the proposed design in 1799, actual work began under the direction of Hübler. Hübler consciously integrated the ruins of the old Cistercian monastery. This creative bridge

to the past corresponded to the taste of garden art at the time, as well as Hübler's favoured implementation of trees and shrubs for contrast. A small English park was created, which could no longer be merely considered a sentimental landscape garden, despite the sensitivity of the location. The chapel was shrouded in a shady grove, in accordance with its solemn function. The purposely-arranged view perspectives within the grounds and into the surrounding landscape are framed by very tall and majestic beeches. They lend an interesting three-dimensional effect and a ceremonial character to the monastery park, essentially limited to the former enclosure and farming areas bordering to the south. Far more ruins were included in the design by Hübler than originally intended. A homogenous and valuable cover of herbs and wild flowers seldom encountered elsewhere, has been preserved in their vicinity. Their spectacular blossoming endows the monastery park with a very special atmosphere in spring. It seems as though liverwort, cowslip and wood anemone, joined by aquilegia, lungwort, larkspur and spiky devil's claw, have been just there since the days of the monastery. A special botanical feature is the brown cranesbill (Geranium phaeum). This plant blossoming in June/July has become widespread in the monastery park.

The old Praying Pillar

Monastery Park in spring with Abbey Ruin, Burial Chapel and Conversion House

Ruin of grain store in the Monastery Park

Palace Gardens Weesenstein

i Schloss Weesenstein
Am Schlossberg 1
01809 Müglitztal
Tel. 03 50 27/6 26 29
Fax 03 50 27/6 26 28
www.schloss-
weesenstein.de
weesenstein@t-online.de

Size of the grounds: 6 ha

⊙ May – October
Daily 9.00 am – 7.00 pm
November–April
Daily 9.00 am – 5.00 pm
24 December closed

✕

P

DB

🚌 Bus

♿ Disabled accessibility

The Palace Gardens Weesenstein date back to the second half of the 16th century, according to the earliest sparse information available. They were established by the House of von Bünau, who ruled Weesenstein for over 360 years, being modified and extended in the course of the centuries in accordance with respective contemporary tastes. The turning point for remodelling and enlargement of the grounds was represented in particular by the family von Uckermann taking power in the year 1772 and the sale of the estate to King Anton of Saxony in 1830. Final significant alterations took place after 1838, under Prince Johann, later King Johann of Saxony. The gardens possess a very special charm, mainly on account of their unusual topography. They seem to be hidden by the imposing palace situated in the narrow Müglitztal and the steep slopes of the foothills of the Erzgebirge mountains. A view of the two regular sections of the gardens separated by the Müglitz, becomes only possible from the palace bridge located 20 m above the valley. At this point, the visitor has to choose whether to visit the palace followed by the gardens, or to first enter the gardens. There is no other path linking the gardens to the palace located on the spur of the mountain. The path to the palace runs next to the Mühlgraben (mill ditch), leading first to the smaller and from there to the larger garden section, all the way to the Baroque garden pavilion located there. The visitor may enjoy a wonderful view of the entire palace ensemble from this point. A second, very large and also Baroque garden pavilion was situated on the mountaintop south of the gatehouse. Few traces remain of the pavilion and its surrounding English sections. The belvedere was pulled down in 1951. The recently conducted revitalisation work on this area, has however uncovered indications of notable garden design features created during the second half of the 18th century.

View from the palace bridge

Fountain in the small palace garden

Garden pavilion in the large palace garden

Miruspark Mildenstein in Leisnig

 Burg Mildenstein
Burglehn 6
04703 Leisnig
Tel. 03 43 21/1 26 52
Fax 03 43 21/5 15 37
www.burg-mildenstein.de
info@burg-mildenstein.de

Size of the grounds: 0.7 ha

April – October
Tues-Sun, Public holidays
9.00 am – 5.00 pm
November
Tues–Fri 9.00 am – 4.00 pm
Sat, Sun, Public holidays
9.00 am – 5.00 pm
24, 25, 31 December closed

P

DB

Bus

Disabled accessibility

Ruin in the Miruspark

Only few remnants of the Miruspark established in the 19th century have remained. The park on the very steep inclines below Castle Mildenstein, created by the finance procurator Benjamin Ehrenfried Mirus and his descendants, is one of the few examples of Romantic landscape garden art of bourgeois origin in Saxony. The largest building of the park is the Neogothic ruin placed ingeniously on the shoulder of the slope. The pieces of work originating from the derelict monastery Buch, an old grave-stone and a 190 year-old robinia, integrated in the building, endow the ensemble with the medieval character popular in the Romantic period. The scenery was formerly enhanced by a knight's stairway with "knights" and a hermit hut with "hermits". Further perspectives open up to views of the valley of the Freiberger Mulde, from the ruin and the paths winding along the incline. The grounds of the Miruspark covered with a carpet of larkspur are particularly attractive in spring.

Castle Gardens Gnandstein

Gardens belonging to Castle Gnandstein in the possession of the family von Einsiedel since the 15ᵗʰ century have been authenticated in the archives since 1638. Specified are a herb garden with fruit trees and a naturally-growing fence, a sloping garden with fruit trees, an onion garden with fruit trees and an orchard with cherry trees. Only the castle gardens have remained out of the gardens located around the castle. They are situated to the south east of the castle complex, and may be recognised from afar on account of its mighty terraced walls. The pleasure garden first mentioned in 1717, is situated on the middle terrace of the castle gardens. The representative access steps first lead to the orangery area, in which the cultivation of rosemary and carnations plays an important role. In future, the adjacent area will feature high espaliers with ancient Saxon varieties of grape vines and different methods of growing espalier fruit. The largest area accommodates the flower and herb gardens.

ⓘ Burg Gnandstein
Burgstraße 3
04655 Kohren-Sahlis
Tel. 03 43 44/6 13 09
Fax 03 43 44/6 13 83
burg.gnandstein@
t-online.de

Size of the grounds: 0.5 ha

☉ January
Sat, Sun 10.00 am – 4.00 pm
February – April, November
Tues – Sun,
10.00 am – 5.00 pm
May – October
Tues – Sun,
10.00 am – 6.00 pm
December
Tues – Sat,
10.00 am – 4.00 pm
Ascension Day,
24, 25, 31 December and
1 January closed

✕ – 🅿 – 🚌 Bus

♿ Disabled accessibility

Pleasure ground terrace

City, palace and park Moritzburg, arieal view

Source of illustrations:
Staatliche Schlösser, Burgen und Gärten Sachsen
Frank Höhler: p. 201, 203, 204, 205, 209, 210, 211, 212/13, 214, 215, 217,
219, 220, 221, 224, 229
Herbert Boswank: p. 202, 207, 230
Udo Pellmann: p. 206
Gabriele Goers: p. 208
Gabriele Hanke: p. 216, 218, 223, 225, 226, 227
Jürgen Karpinski: p. 222
Hans-Dieter Kluge: p. 228
Klaus-Dieter Weber: p. 199

Thuringia

STIFTUNG THÜRINGER SCHLÖSSER UND GÄRTEN

THURINGIAN FOUNDATION OF STATELY HOMES AND GARDENS

STIFTUNG THÜRINGER SCHLÖSSER UND GÄRTEN

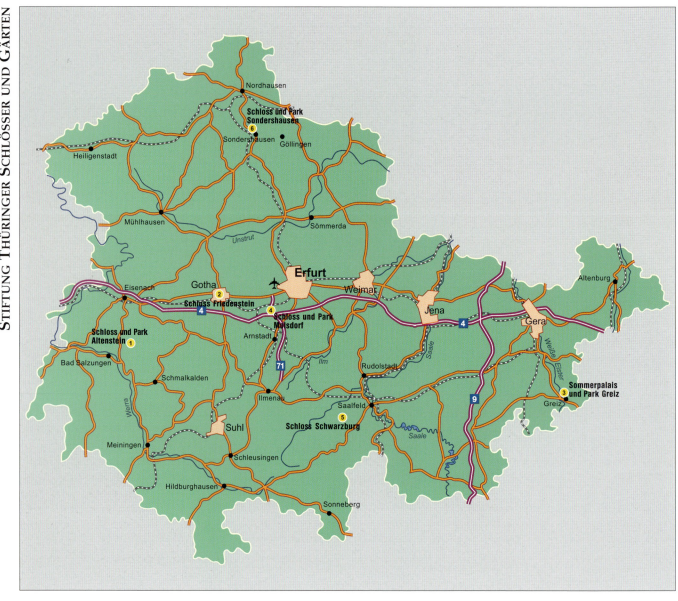

◁ *Parks around Schloss Friedenstein
in Gotha, doric temple, view from
the southwest*

Park Altenstein, palace and basin with fountain, view from the east

THURINGIAN GARDEN LANDSCAPE – GARDEN CULTURE IN CULTIVATED LANDSCAPE

Thuringian garden landscape is one of the richest park landscapes of Germany. Thuringia provides exemplary representatives of a complete cross section of all varieties of architectonic gardens and landscape gardens including all epochs of garden history. Early Renaissance garden art is represented by the partially modified gardens in Schleusingen and Schmalkalden. Basic characteristics of Baroque garden art may be observed in the palaces Schloß Schwarzburg and Schloß Heidecksburg in Rudolstadt. The Baroque basic structure has already been remodelled in the early landscape gardens of Gotha and Molsdorf. Gardens such as the park in Greiz, the palace park in Sondershausen, the landscape gardens of Schloß Altenstein near Bad Liebenstein and the park in Gotha, have finally matured into landscape parks of perfection.

It is the special relationship between garden and landscape, which distinguishes Thuringian garden culture right across the epochs from Renaissance gardens to landscape gardens. Thuringian gardens are no foreign entities within the landscape, but are embedded in a superordinated cultural landscape, which displays features of a park-like nature itself. An individual conservational challenge is presented by the quality of Thuringian gardens as general works of art, as well as the special characteristics of the garden landscape of Thuringia. The gardens, as complete works-of-art, uniting cultivated and natural space, must therefore be the focus of attention in the course of their preservation.

Palace Altenstein, eastern façade

Park Altenstein near Bad Liebenstein

 Schlossverwaltung
(Palace and Castle
Administration)
Schloss und Park Altenstein
36448 Bad Liebenstein
Tel. 03 69 61 / 7 25 13
Fax 03 69 61 / 3 34 08

Size of the grounds: 160 ha

⊙ Park freely accessible

✗

🅿

🚌

*Park Altenstein,
Knight's chapel,
view from the east* ▷

Park Altenstein is one of the most brilliant garden works of art in Thuringia in which park and landscape have merged into one, as so rarely observed in Germany today. Single trees, clusters of trees and forest enclosures divide wide meadow-land, perspectives axes allow a free view of the Werra valley and the distant mountain range of the High Rhön.

The approximately 160 hectare large park near the city Bad Liebenstein owes its existence to the Dukes Georg I, Bernhard II and Georg II of Sachsen-Meiningen. From 1798 onwards, the exceptionally charming topography of the park terrain located on the south-west slopes of the Thuringian Forest, reminiscent of alpine landscapes in a romantic sense, provided Duke Georg I with an opportunity to realise his creative ideas in accordance with the perception of garden art at the close of the 18th century. The love of things Chinese and exotic and the passion for nature based on the ideals of the early Enlightenment, found expression in numerous park architectural objects, as already observed in the landscape gardens of Meining from 1782 onwards. Some of these jewels of garden architecture have been preserved until today,

such as the Neogothic knight's chapel on a steeply jutting out rock behind the palace building, or the Senn (Alpine dairy) hut above the Luisenthaler water-fall, at the sight of which one feels trans-ported to an alpine landscape. Referred to as "Flower Basket", was a copy of a Roman sarcophagus, hewn in stone and planted with flowers, also towering on a steep rock top, but no longer existing today. This solemn sentimental spot was completed by an arch-shaped stone bench at the base of the Flower Basket, and standing behind it until today, a marble bust of Duchess Charlotte Amalie of Sachsen-Meiningen, mother of Georg I, who died in 1801.

Three of the most famous garden artists of Germany were active in Park Alten-stein in the middle of the 19th century under Duke Bernhard II, whose de-signs and recommendations were im-plemented in part. Prince Pückler "advized on the park" in 1845. He super-vised the execution of his suggestions himself, and later, on his recommen-dation, the court gardener of Wei-mar, Carl Eduard Petzold. Petzold sup-plied comprehensive plans for redesign. Results of the activities of Pückler-Petzold

*Park Altenstein,
View of the meadowland
to the north of the palace*

may still be seen in the northern parts of the park.

Paths were set out new and modifications were carried out on the planted areas and woody thickets, in accordance with an improvement plan for the palace environment produced in 1855 by the director general of royal gardens in Prussia Peter Joseph Lennè.

Redesign of the palace terraces and what was referred to as the inner park, the central and most intensively designed area of the park, followed the new construction of the palace from 1888 to 1890 under Duke Georg II. The latter was significantly involved in the design, as can be deduced from letters to the court gardeners and enclosed sketches. Altenstein's large carpet bed and the sumptuously designed creeper entwined palace terraces, acknowledged in many travel reports and professional magazines, corresponded to the taste prevalent at the close of the 19th century.

Parks around Schloss Friedenstein in Gotha

Out of all the gardens established around Schloss Friedenstein in Gotha in the 17th and 18th century, the former "Ducal Park" and "Orangery Gardens" recognisable on account of their independency, have been preserved until today. Together with the Tannengarten (Fir Gardens) created on the grounds of the former kitchen gardens, the Schloßwallgarten (Palace Wall Gardens) and the garden area to the south of the Teeschlößchen (Little Tea Palace), these gardens around Schloss Friedenstein have grown into one large park today.

The Ducal Park, whose creation commenced in 1769, simultaneous to that of the gardens of Wörlitz, is one of the earliest landscape gardens of Thuringia. It was created under direction of the Englishman Haberfield, who came from England to Gotha as a member of the entourage of Ernst, heir to the throne. It is very likely that this particular Haberfield was a member of the gardening family Haverfield in Kew Gardens, since Kew Gardens belonged to the Princess of Wales, who was the aunt of the heir to the throne Ernst, later to be Duke Ernst II of Sachsen-Gotha-Altenburg. A first contemporary description of the Ducal Park may be found in the "Theory of Garden Art" by C.C.L. Hirschfeld from the year 1782, which confirms that exotic woody plants in particular were brought from Kew Gardens to Gotha, and that the gardens offered impressive views of the Thuringian Forest. The contribution of the court gardener Christian Heinrich Wehmeyer, who came from Molsdorf to Gotha in 1772, to the creation and care of the

i Gotha Information
0 36 21 / 22 21 38
www.gotha.de

Size of the grounds: 35 ha

⊘ Park freely accessible

✕

P

DB

Gotha, northeastern orangery building, view from the southwest

Ducal Park, was surely significant. Prince Friedrich honoured Wehmeyer with a memorial in the shape of a tree trunk bearing the respectful inscription "Den Manen des würdigen Wehmeyer" (approximating to: To the Manes of honourable Wehmeyer).

A special feature of the gardens to be noted, is the design of the large artificial park lake, with its island referred to as 'holy' later, which has the effect that the relatively small area of water cannot be taken in by a single glance. The island attained further significance by the burial of Duke Ernst II and other members of the ducal house.

The Orangery Gardens are situated to the east below the palace. They form, flanked by the orangery buildings created after 1747, and together with the court of honour of the neighbouring Schloss Friedrichsthal, a uniform garden area. The original garden designs by the architect Gottfried Heinrich Krohne of a Baroque garden with elaborate parterres were never realised. Orangery plant stocks numbering over 3000 plants were remarkable towards the end of the 18th century, enjoying 'the reputation of being Germany's best'. The present-day appearance of the Orangery Gardens corresponds to the design of 1930.

Gotha, park lake with temple, western bank

Greiz Park

Greiz Park is situated in the western edge of the former seat, or "Residenzstadt", of the Counts and later Princes Reuß Ältere Linie (Reuß Elder Line), in the valley of the White Elster, below the Upper Palace. Its origins go back as far as to the time around 1650, when a pleasance was created in the western region at the bottom of the valley. A small palace complex was built under Count Heinrich II who ruled from 1715 to 1722, the south wing of which housed an extensive collection of orangery plants.

Around 1768/69, Count Heinrich XI had the initial garden palace replaced with a summer palais, based on the French model. The building was positioned in a southerly direction, in order to accommodate the orangery in the ground floor.

The palais known as the "maison de belle retraite" served as private retreat for the Prince.

The gardens of those days occupied only the southern area of today's park. Around 1790, it was divided regularly into a lawn area in front of the palais surrounded by potted plants, centrally located kitchen gardens, and a bosket area to the east of these. The first region of irregular design, with winding paths, was created to the north of the palais.

After floods destroyed the pleasure ground in 1799, Prince Heinrich XIII had the gardens redesigned in the landscape style. He had the gardens extended towards the north up to the rush pond. Numerous coniferous plants were added. A special feature of the park is the

i Stadtverwaltung Greiz
Schlossverwaltung
(Palace and Castle
Administration)
Marstallstraße 6
07973 Greiz
Tel. 0 36 61/70 35 10
Fax 0 36 61/70 35 98

Size of the grounds: 60 ha

☉ Park freely accessible
Guided tour of the Park
Meeting point: Blumenuhr
(Flower clock)
All year round Tues, Thurs
10.00 am, 2.00 pm
and by arrangement

✗ – DB

Double page overleaf:
Greiz Park, view of the park and the city from the White Cross

Greiz Park, rush pond in the park, view from the south

Greiz Park, pleasure ground with summer palais, view from the east

Pinetum north of the summer palais, an accumulation of exotic coniferous plants, and the oldest of their kind in Thuringia. Greiz landscape park was developed further by using plans designed by Johann Michael Sebastian von Riedl engaged at the Viennese court. Rearrangements and new planting based on this, was carried out between 1827 and 1830. The border to the landscape beyond was crossed at this time, with buildings and memorials placed outside the park area, such as the Gasparine Temple or the White Cross.

Plans for a new railway line, which was to bisect the park initially, but was then moved to the eastern edge in 1873, led to renewed changes. The garden director of Muskau Carl Eduard von Petzold produced an overall plan on this occasion, which was implemented by Rudolph Reinecken with modifications during the ensuing decades. The banks of the rush pond were imparted with a more stimulating design, small groves and thickets were redistributed in the meadowlands achieving three-dimensional effects and the curved paths were redesigned more generously. The limited planting of flowers remained reserved to the palace environs. One of the most significant landscape parks of the 19th century was created in Thuringia, visually integrating the entire river valley and harmonically enhancing the natural landscape.

◁ *Greiz Park, view of the pleasure ground*

Molsdorf Park, view from the palace to south

Molsdorf Palace Park

View of the southern façade of the palace ▷

i Schlossverwaltung
Schloss Molsdorf
(Palace and Castle
Administration)
Schlossplatz 6
99192 Molsdorf
Tel. 03 62 02 / 22 0 85
Fax 03 62 02 / 22 0 84

Size of the grounds: 8 ha

⊙ Park freely accessible

✕

🅿

🚌

The Baroque Palace Molsdorf and its park, originally a Wasserburg (moated castle) is situated in Molsdorf near Erfurt. After having purchased this estate in 1734, the Reichsgraf (Imperial Count) Gustav Adolph von Gotter completed the regular gardens initiated in 1716 by the previous owner, Counsellor Schultze from Hannover. Gotter was able to continue the creation of gardens containing "walks", espaliers, canals and 'water art', as well as a diverse assortment of fruit trees and small pyramidal plane trees. Gotter brought these Baroque gardens to the peak of their creative design. The gardens obtained their "royal appearance" by virtue of broderie parterres, boskets, berceaux and water artwork (berceaux = pergola walks), as well as an extensive orangery and luxurious sculptural embellishments.

After the ducal house of Sachsen-Gotha-Altenburg took over palace and gardens in 1762, the first simplifications and partial dissolution of the regular structure were carried out towards the end of the 18th century. The gardens were finally redesigned into a landscape park in the 20's of the 19th century, without however completely abandoning the basic Baroque layout. Rudolph Eyserbeck, son of the famous gardener of Wörlitz Johann Friedrich Eyserbeck, is credited with this achievement, after having been court gardener in Molsdorf since 1788 and being appointed chief court gardener of Gotha in 1814.
Up to this day, Molsdorf has been virtually completely preserved as a charming example of a synthesis of regular architectural and landscape garden art.

Molsdorf Park, male figure with lion (Hercules)

The Pleasure Ground of Palace Schwarzburg

The creation of pleasance and Kaisersaal (Emperor's Hall) of Schloss Schwarzburg is connected to the elevation of the Counts of Schwarzburg to the rank of Reichsfürsten (Imperial Princes) in 1697. A new garden house was initially erected in 1699 on the garden terrace created as a result of fire damage in 1695, the shell of the orangery building being completed by 1709. The diplomatic measures preceding the elevation in rank in 1709/10 included luxurious refurbishment of the Emperor's Hall and upgrading to temple of honour with regard to the royal descent of the House of Schwarzburg. Ludwig Friedrich of Schwarzburg-Rudolstadt accepted the hereditary tribute as Prince, in Schloss Schwarzburg as early as 1710. Work on the new pleasure ground commenced immediately afterwards, being completed in 1719, with the rest of the complex.

The ground floor of the Emperor's Hall building, especially the sala terrena below the Emperor's Hall, served as greenhouse winter domicile for the garden's potted plants. The Emperor's Hall was thus a building connected to the pleasure ground, serving simultaneously as orangery, summerhouse, temple of honour and garden house. The Baroque gardens, which were included in the original garden layout plans of 1744, essentially consisted of a lawn square with crossroads and central fountain. The square of lawn was decorated with garden figures including allegories of the seven free arts and the four humours as well as potted plants from the orangery. A broderie area was created in front of the Emperor's Hall building on the occasion of the marriage of Johann Friedrich and Bernhardine Christiane Sophie of Schwarzburg-Rudolstadt in 1744, which however, disappeared again quickly. A space for arranging the orangery plants has been designated there since the restoration of

i Schlossverwaltung (Palace and Castle Administration) Schloss Heidecksburg 07407 Rudolstadt Tel./Fax 03672/447210

Size of the grounds: 0.3 ha

⊙ Palace gardens freely accessible

✕ In town

🅿

DB

Double page overleaf: Palace Schwarzburg, lawn parterre and Emperor's Hall from the south

Palace Schwarzburg, view from the south (aerial view)

the pleasure ground in 2001. The bosket area to the south of the parterre, of which there is evidence dating back to the Baroque period, has been reconstructed as a grove of trees in 2001.

The special feature of the pleasure ground of Schwarzburg, is the close association of the orangery gardens with the iconographic programme of the Emperor's Hall. The citrus tree is stylised as the family tree of Schwarzburg by means of allegorical and metaphoric references, thus representing pictorially the ancient honourable descent of this lineage and its royal claim. Since the restoration of the elements of the orangery in 2001, it is now once more possible to fully experience this general work of art.

Palace Schwarzburg, garden parterre with fountain basin and symmetrical grove of trees, view from the north

Sondershausen Palace Park

Simultaneous to the erection of the palace complex in Sondershausen from the 16th century, the first gardens were established to the west, with the chief purpose of providing supplies for the court kitchen. Appointment of a court gardener is recorded from 1533.

The gardens were extended and re-designed around 1700. A house referred to as Achteckhaus (Octagonal House), which accommodated a carousel, was constructed in 1709/10 at the end of a hedge-lined maille alley. A clipped avenue linked the pheasantry created in the "Loh" (Lohe is the bark used for tanning) in 1694, with the garden area on the palace hill. Two pairs of obelisks stood at the beginning and end of this avenue exactly aligned towards the palace tower. One of the preserved obelisks bears the initials of Prince Christian Wilhelm of Schwarzburg-Sondershausen and the tools of the gardeners' guild.

Under garden inspector Dr. Tobias Ekart, work to change and redesign the palace park began in 1837, concentrating at first on the area below the palace hill towards the Wipper and the Lohplatz. It was Ekart's idea, which he expressed in his "Contemplations on creative landscape garden art in an explanatory description of the Princely Park of Sondershausen" in 1840, that the creation of the palace park should include a public garden as part of an all-embracing beautification of the land. The creation of an extensive landscape garden began in the Wipper valley, with two park lakes, numerous, curvaceous footpaths and carriageways, open meadowland and forest-like groves. Ekart wanted to set representative highlights with the flower gardens created near the Prince's palais and the new pleasure ground planned to the west of the Octagonal House. His work was however repeatedly halted by terrible flooding of the Wipper.

The pheasantry in the Lohplatz was redesigned around 1800, with a firing range, a drinking hall, and a building with a recess specifically for the accommodation of the Guards Music Corps. This is where the public "Loh music" came into existence, on which Sondershausen's reputation as a city of music is founded.

i Schlossverwaltung
Schloss Sondershausen
99706 Sondershausen
Tel. 0 36 32 / 66 30
Fax 0 36 32 / 66 31 04

Size of the grounds: 30 ha

⊙ Park freely accessible

Sondershausen Palace, garden layout design (Petzold plan from 1851)

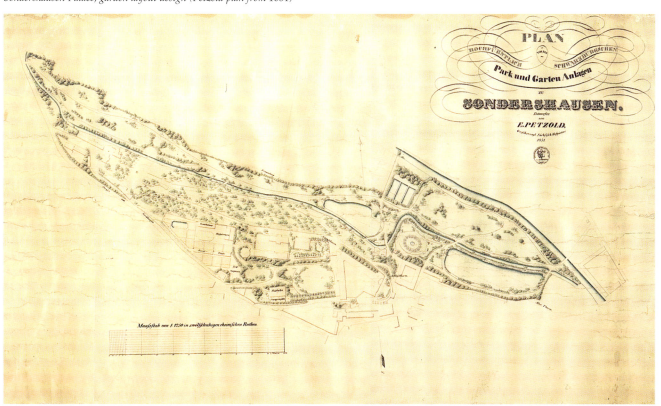

Sondershausen Park, view of the large park lake to the west

Sondershausen Park, obelisk at the palace drive from Lohplatz

Differences between Ekart and the Hof-marschall's office (equivalent to the lord chamberlain) resulted in Ekart requesting his retirement in 1847. The court gardener of Weimar of that time, Carl Eduard Petzold was commissioned to continue with the design of the park. Execution of his proposed design modifications of Ekart's gardens, was taken on by Carl Arlt, who was appointed royal chief gardener in 1852, and garden director in 1872.

Restoration of the palace park, damaged severely during the war and post-war period, has been in progress for several years.

Sondershausen palace, west wing and pleasure ground

STIFTUNG THÜRINGER SCHLÖSSER UND GÄRTEN

Rudolstadt

i Palace Heidecksburg
07407 Rudolstadt
Tel./Fax 03672/447210

Schmalkalden

i Palace Wilhelmsburg
98574 Schmalkalden
Tel./Fax 03683/401976

Schleusingen

i Palace Bertholdsburg
98553 Schleusingen
Tel. 036841/531214
Fax 036841/531227

Source of illustrations:
Stiftung Thüringer Schlösser und Gärten, Helmut Wiegel: p. 231, 233, 235, 236, 237, 238, 239, 242, 243, 245, 246, 248/49, 250, 252 unten
Stiftung Thüringer Schlösser und Gärten, Constantin Beyer: p. 234, 240/41, 244, 246, 252 oben
Stiftung Thüringer Schlösser und Gärten, Catrin Lorenz: p. 253
Ralf Kruse & Thomas Seidel GbR, Weinböhla: p. 247
Foto-Lösche, Rudolstadt: p. 251

INDEX OF PLACES

INDEX OF NAMES AND OBJECTS

Staatliche Schlösser und Gärten
Baden-Württemberg
(Public Stately Homes and Gardens
of Baden-Württemberg)

Baden
Oberfinanzdirektion Karlsruhe
Moltkestraße 50
76133 Karlsruhe
Tel. 07 21/9 26-0
Fax 07 21/9 26-65 70
www.schloesser-und-gaerten.de

Württemberg
Oberfinanzdirektion Stuttgart
Postfach 103641
70031 Stuttgart
Tel. 07 11/66 73-0
Fax 07 11/66 73-35 34

**Bayerische Verwaltung der Staatlichen
Schlösser Gärten und Seen
(Bavarian Administration
of Public Stately Homes, Gardens
and Lakes)**
Schloss Nymphenburg, Eingang 16
80638 München
Tel. 0 89/1 79 08-0
Fax 0 89/1 79 08-154
www.schloesser.bayern.de

**Stiftung Preussische Schlösser
und Gärten Berlin-Brandenburg
(Berlin-Brandenburg Foundation of
Prussian Stately Homes and Gardens)**
Postfach 601462
14414 Potsdam
Tel. 03 31/96 94-0
Fax 03 31/96 94-106
www.spsg.de

**Kulturstiftung DessauWörlitz
(DessauWörlitz Cultural Foundation)**
Schloss Großkühnau
06846 Dessau
Tel. 03 40/6 46 15-0
Fax 03 40/6 46 15-10
www.ksdw.de

**Verwaltung der Staatlichen Schlösser
und Gärten Hessen
(Administration of Public Stately
Homes and Gardens in Hessen)**
Schloss
61348 Bad Homburg v.d. Höhe
Tel. 0 61 72/9262-00
Fax 0 61 72/9262-190
www.schloesser-hessen.de

**Burgen, Schlösser, Altertümer
Rheinland-Pfalz
(Castles, Stately Homes and Ancient
Sites of Rhineland-Palatinate)**
Festung Ehrenbreitstein
56077 Koblenz
Tel. 02 61/9 74 24-0
Fax 02 61/9 74 24-50
www.burgen-rlp.de

**Staatliche Schlösser, Burgen
und Gärten Sachsen
(Public Stately Homes, Castles
and Gardens of Saxony)**
Stauffenbergallee 2
01099 Dresden
Tel. 03 51/8 27-46 01
Fax 03 51/8 27-46 02
www.schloesser.sachsen.de

**Stiftung Thüringer Schlösser
und Gärten
(Thuringian Foundation of
Stately Homes and Gardens)**
Postfach 100142
07391 Rudolstadt
Tel. 03672/447-0
Fax 0372/447-119
www.ThueringerSchloesser.de